Pressed Glass

Other Titles in the Warner Collector's Guides Series

Available Now

The Warner Collector's Guide to
Pressed Glass

Lawrence Grow

*Photographs by Peter Ferencze
and Mark Walker*

A Main Street Press Book

A Warner Communications Company

Copyright © 1982 by The Main Street Press
All rights reserved

Warner Books, Inc.
75 Rockefeller Plaza
New York, NY 10019

 A Warner Communications Company

Printed in the United States of America

First printing, June 1982

10 9 8 7 6 5 4 3 2 1

Library of Congress Cataloging in Publication Data

Grow, Lawrence.
  The Warner collector's guide to pressed glass.

  (The Warner collector's guides)
  Bibliography: p. 253
  Includes index.
  1. Pressed glass—United States—Collectors and
collecting. I. Title. II. Series.
NK5203.D3   748.2913   81-3038
ISBN 0-446-97709-8 (USA)   AACR2
ISBN 0-446-37089-4 (Canada)

Contents

How To Use This Book

The purpose of this book is to provide the collector with a visual identification guide to 19th-century American pressed glass. To this end, an attempt has been made to classify pieces by their form rather than by pattern, the usual procedure in more advanced texts. The experienced collector may already know something of forms and patterns; the beginner is likely to recognize only a few designs and to concentrate, instead, on forms. The fifty categories in this easy-to-use guide, therefore, present a broad perspective and provide even the most inexperienced collector with an overview of the wide range of pressed glass objects available. The categories chosen for inclusion are those which are most frequently encountered today. This guide is, of necessity, selective. Millions of pieces of pressed glass were produced from the late 1820s through the first years of the 20th century. To catalogue every possible variety—including one-of-a-kind pieces—would necessitate a multivolume work requiring a lifetime of effort.

Use of this collector's guide is designed with ease and portability in mind. Suppose you spot an unidentified dish at a flea market or in an antiques shop. Perhaps the dealer has told you the seemingly obvious: "It is a piece of Victorian pressed pattern glass." By flicking his finger against the rim, he may demonstrate from the resulting ring that the piece is or is not flint glass. But what kind of piece is it? By turning to the Color Key (pp. 17-48), you are likely to find among the fifty color illustrations a photograph of a dish that bears a close "family resemblance" to the one you're interested in—the visible characteristics, the basic shape, are definitely similar. Under the color illustration will be found the name of the classification and the number of the chapter in the guide that discusses and illustrates dishes in that category. By turning to these pages, you will be able to study other similar pieces, to learn more about their common shapes and patterns, makers, and composition.

Use of this collector's guide is designed with ease and portability in mind. Suppose you spot an unidentified dish at a flea market or in an antiques shop. Perhaps the dealer has told you the seemingly obvious: "It is a piece of Victorian pressed pattern glass." By flicking his finger against the rim, he may demonstrate from the resulting ring that the piece is or is not flint glass. But what kind of piece is it? By turning to the Color Key (pp. 17-48), you are likely to find among the fifty color illustrations a photograph of a dish that bears a close "family resemblance" to the one you're interested in—the visible characteristics, the basic shape, are definitely similar. Under the color illustration will be found the name of the classification and the number of the chapter in the guide that discusses and illustrates dishes in that category. By turning to these pages, you will be able to study other similar pieces, to learn more about their common shapes and patterns, makers, and composition.

Using this guide, then, is very simple. To repeat: once you find a piece that you want to find out more about, turn to the Color Key (pp. 17-48), find the color photograph that most closely identifies the classification of your object, and turn to the chapter for further information.

Each of the approximately 500 pieces discussed in this guide is treated in a separate numbered entry, containing basic information. A typical entry is reproduced on p. 9, together with a list of all the usual elements contained in every entry of the book, from date and maker (if known), to pattern and source. Detailed information on the piece or pieces illustrated in the color plate is given immediately following the category introduction. Most of these elements are self-explanatory, but three require a word of introduction.

Maker: Most pressed glass is not marked. At least the early pieces, however, have been thoroughly studied over the years, and much of this production can be identified by factory. For further discussion of this problem, please consult the Introduction. The location of the company is given each time, if known, with the exception of the Boston and Sandwich Glass Co. The Sandwich, Mass., site is too well known to be repeated **ad infinitum.**

Date or period: It is very difficult to precisely date a given piece. Even those designs which were patented may defy exact placement in time since patterns were often marketed long before and after patent protection was granted. If sales catalogue records exist, a closer approximation of a date is possible, but few pieces were marketed for only a year or two. Since the same mold was likely to have been used over and over again, the most accurate dating probably encompasses only a period—a decade or two.

Patterns: Numerous works are devoted to documenting the enormous variety of patterns and bodies produced during both the flint and non-flint glass periods. As noted in the Introduction, names vary from authority to authority. If there is a choice to be made, the name given in Ruth Webb Lee's **Early American Pressed Glass** has been selected. To aid the reader in identifying cup plate designs, references are given to illustrations in **American Glass Cup Plates** by Ruth Webb Lee and James H. Rose. Other entries contain references to Alice Hulett Metz's **Early American Pattern Glass** volumes, to Helen and George McKearin's classic **American Glass,** and to **American Pressed Glass and Figure Bottles** by Albert Christian Revi.

A Typical Entry

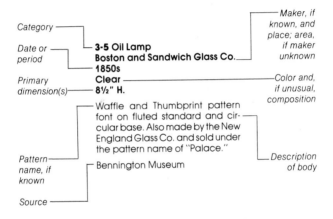

Category

Date or period

Primary dimension(s)

Pattern name, if known

Source

3-5 Oil Lamp
Boston and Sandwich Glass Co.
1850s
Clear
8½" H.

Waffle and Thumbprint pattern font on fluted standard and circular base. Also made by the New England Glass Co. and sold under the pattern name of "Palace."

Bennington Museum

Maker, if known, and place; area, if maker unknown

Color and, if unusual, composition

Description of body

Acknowledgments

The active assistance of students, collectors, and dealers of American pressed glass has been indispensable in preparing this book for publication. The difficult job of selecting representative pieces from the Bennington Museum collection was made much easier with the help of Ruth Levin, registrar, and Eugene R. Kosche, senior curator. Thanks to the interest of David W. Dangremond, director and chief curator of the museum, the collection was open for examination and photography over a period of four months in 1981.

Among the dealers and collectors who have generously shared their expertise and enthusiasm are Nancy Olsson, Durham, Pa.; James D. Tyler, Frenchtown, N.J.; James Robertson and Donald Thornton, Doylestown, Pa.; and Renee Spector, Newtown, Pa.

About the Bennington Museum

The Bennington Museum, incorporated in 1876, houses a collection of more than 7,000 pieces of blown, blown-molded, and pressed glass, primarily of American origin. Together these examples form a comprehensive collection which displays the stylistic changes and technological advancements of two centuries of American glassmaking. Several important private collections have formed the nucleus of the museum's holdings of New England, Mid-Atlantic, and Midwestern 19th-century glass. These include the Stanley B. Ineson collection of early American blown glass; the Rev. and Mrs. Richard Allen Day collection of mercury glass; and the Channing Hare-Montford Coolidge, Ralph Edwards, and Gertrude B. Webster collections. Late-19th- and early-20th-century art glass is well-represented by the Joseph W. and May K. Limric collection.

Two important study collections are also available to students and collectors. The Norman A. MacColl collection of pressed glass goblets includes 1,242 different patterns. The Burton Gates study collection includes more than 2,000 glass fragments dug at the site of the Sandwich Glass Co. factory in 1914.

The Bennington Museum, one of America's outstanding regional museums, is located on West Main Street (Route 9) in Bennington, Vermont. The museum is open to the public seven days a week from March 1st to the end of November.

Introduction

Pressed glass is eminently collectible because so much of value in this medium has been produced over the past 150 years in the United States. Of all the decorative arts, pressed glass is perhaps the most American in expression and technique. Although the method of pressing was developed concurrently in Europe during the early 1800s, American inventiveness in meeting the need for decorative but practical objects for the home is unquestioned. While European glassmakers excelled at the production of finer specialty wares—especially those which are cut or engraved—their counterparts here pursued a much broader course. The technique of pressing a batch of molten liquid in a mold rapidly evolved from a quite primitive operation devoted to the production of a few items—among them cup plates, lamp bases, and salts—to the widespread manufacture of sets of tableware and other household articles. And even though the pressing method does not allow for as much individual expression as do the various techniques of blowing glass, many early pressed wares made in this country—whether of a flint or a non-flint composition—have a distinct character of their own.

The scope of this book has been defined as the period of years during which craftmanship was generally at its best—from the late 1820s to the early 1900s. This is basically the Victorian age in America, a more complex period, both technically and stylistically, than the provincial which preceded it or the modern which followed. Lacy designs of the 1830s and '40s have little in common with the naturalistic patterns of twenty years later. What objects in both styles may share is a boldness of line, a brilliance of "metal," as glassmakers have traditionally termed the medium in which they work, and weight. It is generally recognized that flint glass pieces made through the 1860s are superior in execution to the non-flint of succeeding years. This is a common judgement, however, which is just as commonly invalidated. The lime glass formula which came into widespread use in the 1870s by no means rendered pressed glass objects less desirable in design or execution. Patterns were often pressed with more precision than they were in earlier years, and while the weight of the average piece declined with the elimination of flint, the loss of substance may not be great.

Not included in this book are the so-called carnival and Depression wares, the pressed glass of the 1920s and '30s which is so highly sought today. There is no denying its popularity; the glass is widely available and, therefore, prices are still reasonable for most varieties. By no means, however, can one argue that the design is as imaginative and well-executed as that found throughout much of the 19th-century ware. Carnival glass is a less expensive form of blown art glass; Depression glass is distinguished primarily for its color—soft green, blue, pink, a strong amber—and not because of any pressed pattern. Both types of 20th-century glass have been well-documented in books and articles and do not require further exposition.

Objects made in the early 20th century are, however, included in this book. In style, they look back to the previous decades. The United States Glass Company, the mammoth Pittsburgh conglomerate formed from the merger of eighteen western Pennsylvania, Ohio, and West

Virginia firms in 1891, revived old patterns in the 1890s and in the first decade of the 20th century.

The glass collection of the Bennington Museum, an institution better known for its extraordinary pottery wares, is increasingly being recognized as a major resource for students and collectors. Formed under the guidance of Richard Carter Barret, the collection of 19th- and early-20th century American blown and pressed glass has been added to on a continual basis. It now includes representative examples of nearly every type of pressed ware made until the 1920s. Also found in the collection are a number of exceptional objects, most of which are products of the Sandwich or New England Glass Co. factories during the 1840s and '50s.

Only selected examples from the Bennington collection have been published to date, this volume being the first to survey it in its entirety. The collector is likely to find these examples quite typical of the kind of objects to be found today in private hands. There is, however, a much higher representation of New England pieces in the Bennington collection than those made in the Pittsburgh area or the Midwest. Collectors all over the county, rightly or wrongly, have always favored pressed glass made in the East. In order to present as wide a variety of objects as possible, the Bennington examples have been supplemented in this book with some privately owned pieces.

The term "Sandwich" is one that has caused much confusion. For many years it was used loosely to describe almost any kind of lacy or non-lacy pressed object made from the 1820s through the '50s or '60s. Despite the best efforts of the experts, the practice continues today. Thanks to the research of Lowell Innes and other students of the Pittsburgh-area glass factories, we now know that much that was considered singularly Sandwich or New England in origin could have been produced elsewhere. One must say "could" rather than "was" in many instances because pressed glass usually defies exact attribution. It is, unlike many of the other decorative arts, one of the most anonymous in execution. Sales catalogues, fragments found on the site of an old factory, and production records sometimes can be marshaled in support of particular claims, but this is often the exception. Patterns were copied widely and one version is frequently mistaken for another. A manufacturer's mark or impress is a great rarity usually found only on very early work.

The beginning collector will find it very difficult, then, to identify the work of a particular company or to substantiate a claim made by others. There are, however, stylistic differences which emerge upon close examination of similar pieces such as cup plates and candlesticks (and other forms) made before the pattern glass period of 1850-90. The pattern-glass objects, usually made up as parts of sets, are somewhat easier to identify, but, as noted earlier, one must look carefully for the subtle differences. There is some evidence that molds used in pressing were sometimes supplied by one company to another, but even when this was the case, the execution of the pattern and form is likely to be marked by some slight differences.

Pattern names can be very confusing. An index of those used in this book is included to make cross-reference comparison easier. Most of the original trade names have disappeared and were replaced with more visually descriptive terms by 20th-century collectors. The same pattern may be known one way in the East and termed something else in the Midwest. When there has been a choice to make, the name given in Ruth Webb Lee's **Early American Pressed Glass** has been selected.

The serious collector will learn something of the technical development of the pressed glass industry—from the late 1820s until at least the adoption of the lime glass formula in the 1860s and '70s. The story is basically one of a small industry based primarily in the East which began producing pressed ware along with blown and blown-molded pieces. Within a generation, the technology of mold making, of shaping the molten liquid more precisely, of firing the pressed piece to a satisfactory brilliance, had been greatly improved. By the Civil War, the center of production had begun to shift to the Pittsburgh and Wheeling region, and a highly sophisticated level of manufacture, an almost standardized degree of mass production, was coming into being. It was then that the more pliant and less expensive lime glass formula was adopted for pattern wares.

The earlier flint glass was often crudely made. As Lura Woodside Watkins has accurately observed: "It was full of bubbles, grit, and lumps of quartz. Much of it was off-color. That these irregularities endear it to the collector does not alter the facts." The elaborate lacy patterns, born of the need to cover up imperfections, served a useful purpose in the 1830s and '40s. The stippling produced a faceted effect not unlike that seen in cut glass, and lent a brilliance to an otherwise cloudy surface. The "irregularities" are found as often in pieces produced in the East as those made in the Pittsburgh area at the same time, although the early Eastern output is generally recognized as being finer in execution than the Pittsburgh of Midwestern because of the use of better molds.

Pressed glass of the 1850s through the '90s is of a much purer, cleaner composition, whether flint or non-flint. The former is usually recognized as being more brilliant, having a harder, weightier substance which effectively captures light. Every collector of flint ware soon learns to test a piece for a bright, bell-like tone by tapping its edge. The crystal of the late century, however, compares favorably in both tone and brilliance.

The collector will also find that the variety of forms available in later ware is much greater than it was in earlier years. The first sets of tableware may have consisted of only five or six kinds of objects—a cream pitcher, sugar bowl, celery vase, compote, and goblets and wines. The extent of production gradually broadened during the century to include many items—cups and mugs, trays, jars—which previously had been available principally in various metals and alloys, or in pottery and porcelain. Pattern ware sets may be made up of as many as twenty-five types of dishes, a great variety of drinking glasses, and such special containers as jars for condiments, a molasses or syrup jug, or a punch bowl set with cups. Because so wide a diversity of objects was produced in clearly defined pattern sets, the collecting of this type of mid-to-late-Victorian ware is far more popular than the collecting of lacy or non-pattern glass.

Concurrent with the development of pattern wares was the shift in the center of production to the Midwest, including such states as Ohio and Indiana, in addition to western Pennsylvania and West Virginia. Many of the old firms in this region had followed styles set in the East, adopting patterns at will to fit their own purposes. In the 1870s and '80s, however, a more enterprising spirit was expressed in the production of such unusual bodies as marble glass, and opal ware or milk glass. Frosted ware had been popular since the 1860s, and later iridescent and flashed or stained effects also caught the public's fancy. The Eastern factories did not lag far behind in new decorative techniques, but a clear lead was taken by such firms as Challinor,

Taylor and Co., Richards and Hartley; Atterbury and Co.; and Doyle and Co.—all of the Pittsburgh area. There was also much experimentation with unusual and often whimsical forms: mustard pots in the form of a small turkey, covered dishes shaped as a rabbit or hen, serving dishes in the outline of a fish.

Pinpointing the period when pressed glass was best produced will always be a matter of argument among collectors. Clearly, by the time of the United States Glass Co. merger, the halcyon days had passed. Pattern ware had become so common and commercial, so successfully merchandised, that a sort of aesthetic boredom set in. The discerning public was now much more interested in cut glass and in blown art glass. But not surprisingly at this time, there was the beginning of a revivial of enthusiasm for the first, so-called "Colonial" products of the early glass factories, of such firms as Sandwich; New England Glass; Bakewell, Pears and Co.; Union Glass Co.; the Brooklyn Flint Glass Works; and the Jersey Glass Co. Lacy pieces, invariably termed Sandwich, were avidly sought after in the first half of the 20th century. So, too, were the simpler geometric-patterned colored and opaque wares of the 1840s and '50s.

Now, at last, the ambitiously patterned and imaginatively formed objects of the 1860s through the '90s have returned to popularity among collectors. The Metropolitan Museum has recently licensed a reproduction of an 1870s Three-Face pattern candlestick, covered bisquit jar, compote, cake stand, and champagne glass; they share equal billing with reproductions of M'Kee and Co.'s earlier flint Bellflower pattern, Sandwich's "Blackberry," and a selection of lacy dishes and plates. Fortunately for the collector, all of these pieces are clearly marked as to origin. The same, sadly, can not be said for most other reproductions—whether of the early 1900s or the more recent past. Because of its relative anonymity, the pressed glass field is plagued with copies. Those of the late-Victorian variety will surely increase in number.

There are no sure and simple quidelines to follow in authenticating a piece of 19th-century pressed glass. Comparing a piece to a documented example is the safest, but not necessarily the easiest route to follow. It is best to begin collecting on a limited scale—with one pattern or type—and to study its execution with care. Examine the shape of a shaft or stem, look carefully to see how a rim is formed, test the weight of a piece, as well as its tone. Is the color typical? Count the decorative motifs and trace their outlines. Measure a piece. Does it match in size the known examples published in such basic works as those of Ruth Webb Lee and Helen and George McKearin?

Eventually one develops a sixth sense about what is right and wrong. The exact identity of the maker may forever elude the best efforts of the connoisseur. Dates, too, may remain inexact. The question of just when production of a certain piece began and ceased will occupy the attention of scholars for years to come. Of much greater importance is the certainty that a piece is of its period, that it has antique value. And in that determination, there is no substitute for experience.

Color Key to Pressed Glass

1. Miniature Lamps and Chamber Lamps

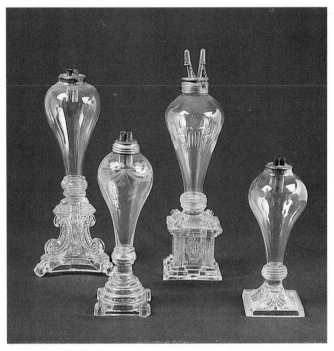

2. Standard Lamps, Pressed and Blown or Blown-Molded

3. Standard Lamps, Pressed

4. Vases

5. Candlesticks, Pressed and Blown or Blown-Molded

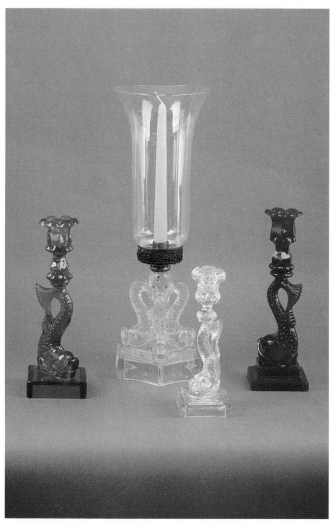

6. Candlesticks, Pressed

7. Spill Holders

8. Furniture Knobs, Doorknobs, Pulls, and Tiebacks

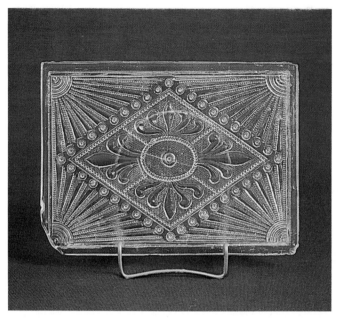

9. Window Glass

10. Salts, Lacy

11. Salts, Solid Color

12. Cup Plates, Historical Designs

13. Cup Plates, Geometric Designs

14. Cup Plates, Representational Designs

15. Entrée Dishes

16. Animal-Form Dishes

17. Sauce, Relish, Honey, and Cheese Dishes

18. Sauce Dishes, Footed

19. Butter Dishes

20. Serving Plates and Platters

21. Standard Plates

22. Trays

23. Cake Stands

24. Compotes and Sweetmeats

25. Celery Vases

26. Pitchers

27. Syrups

28. Cream Pitchers

29. Sugar Bowls

30. Finger Bowls

31. Punch Bowls

32. Bowls

33. Berry Dishes

34. Cups and Mugs

35. Egg Cups

36. Jars

37. Shakers

38. Toothpick Holders and Match Holders

39. Spoon Holders

40. Cruets and Bottles

41. Tumblers

42. Goblets

43. Champagnes and Clarets

44. Wines

45. Ale Glasses and Mugs

46. Whiskey Tasters, Flips, and Tumblers

47. Boudoir Accessories

48. Pomade Jars

49. Novelties

50. Miniatures

1 | Miniature Lamps and Chamber Lamps

Small lighting fixtures that can be carried easily from room to room have been made for hundreds of years. Only in the 19th century, however, did it become common for glass to be used for these objects. With the advent of whale oil as a fuel, special containers were needed that would provide a reservoir and that could be fitted with a burner. From the 1820s on, the first pressed glass manufacturers in New England and the Pittsburgh area sought to provide lamps which were both attractive and useful for everyday purposes. The first small lamps were designed to be carried to the bedchamber. These were not mere miniatures, but eminently practical fixtures which contained enough oil or burning fluid for the short period needed before sleep. As illustrated in 1-1 and 1-4, these are most likely to be handled lamps. Later in the century, when kerosene came into common use, true miniatures—almost exact copies of full-scale lighting fixtures—appeared on the market. Lamps such as those illustrated in 1-0 and 1-5 were permanently stationed on a night table. Most of these fixtures feature naturalistic designs rather than the relatively straight-forward geometric patterns found earlier in the century. The lamps are as frilly, and often as pretty, as the other appointments in a late-Victorian boudoir. While many late kerosene lamps can be found easily today, these miniatures are almost as difficult to discover as the heavier flint glass whale oil fixtures of the first half of the century.

1-O Miniature Oil Lamp (color plate)
Westmoreland Specialty Co., Grapeville, Pa., 1880s
Clear, non-flint
8½" H. to top of chimney; shade, 4½" D.

A miniature oil lamp with an embossed design called "Daisy" is shown in the Westmoreland 1890 catalogue; the design is now termed "Cosmos." The same model was often painted and came in milk glass rather than clear. Nutmeg brass burner.

Ren's Antiques
Newtown, Pa.

1-1 Chamber Lamp
Maker unknown
Mid-1800s
6" H. to top of wicks

Paneled Ovals design; hexagonal, with stepped base. Brass fluid burner and collar.

Bennington Museum

1-2 Chamber Lamp
Boston and Sandwich Glass Co.
1850s
Clear
10¼" H. to top of chimney; 3¾" H.
to top of collar

Early Moon and Star pattern; molded handle. Not to be confused with a later (1880s, Pittsburgh) pattern produced in clear or frosted glass.

Bennington Museum

1-3 Handled Oil Lamp
Maker unknown, Mid-1800s
Clear
3½" H. to collar; base, 4" D.

Plain chamber lamp with pressed sunburst design on bottom of base; brass collar and molded handle.

Ren's Antiques
Newtown Pa.

1-4 Handled Oil Lamp

Maker unknown, Late 1800s
Clear, non-flint
5¾" H. to collar; base, 3¾" D.

Bull's-Eye and Fan pattern; scalloped base and brass collar.

Ren's Antiques
Newtown, Pa.

1-5 Miniature Lamp
Attributed to Butler Bros.
(location unknown), c. 1912
Clear, non-flint
8¾" H. to top of chimney; font,
3¼" D.

Bull's-Eye design in the font; scalloped base and paneled stem. Described in Butler Bros. 1912 catalogue as ''Our Drummer'' model with ''large bull's-eye foot and shoulder, colonial stem.'' Brass burner stem marked ''P & A Mfg. Co.''

Ren's Antiques
Newtown, Pa.

2 | Standard Lamps, Pressed and Blown or Blown-Molded

The first standard whale oil or burning fluid lamps for everyday use in the parlor or dining room were made in two parts—the base and font. As is evident from the color illustration, the base was pressed and the font was blown-molded. This combination of techniques continued to be used long after it was technically possible to press a lamp in one piece. The bases of both lacy and non-lacy lamps made during the 1830-60 period are often extraordinarily beautiful creations. They provide a handsome footing for the airy, teardrop-shaped fonts, many of which incorporate engraving or a delicate overlay pattern. Cup plates were used as bases on some of the earliest of these combined fixtures, and these are extremely rare today. The way in which the font and the base are joined is one of the special characteristics of early lamps. The two elements might be brought together with a thin wafer or ring of blown glass or a knob (knop). The knop, sometimes melon-shaped or hexagonal in form (as were many of the bases), catches the light in a brilliant manner. The shaft or standard of later pressed and blown-molded lamps—which probably burned kerosene—is likely to be less dazzling. Brass ferrules were used to join the two parts as they are in 2-3, 2-4, and 2-5. What later lamps lose in brilliance, however, they often make up in color. The early lamps are most often clear, while those from the 1850s on frequently make use of opaque colors and, as in the Sandwich example illustrated in 2-4, shading or overlay. The "Bride's" or "Marriage Lamp" made by Ripley and Co., 2-6, brings together opaque blue and clambroth.

2-O Whale Oil Lamp (color plate, left to right)
Maker unknown, New England Area, 1840s-50s
Clear
10⅝"

Blown font and pressed, scrolled tripod base with claw feet; ring knop and tin collar.

Whale Oil Lamp
Maker unknown, Pittsburgh area, 1840s-50s
8½" H.

Teardrop-shaped blown font and pressed, fluted base consisting of circle and stepped square; copper wheel engraving on font.

Fluid Lamp
Maker unknown, New England area, 1830s-40s
Clear
11¾" H.

Blown font and Lion and Basket of Flowers pedestal base; ring knop.

Whale Oil Lamp
Attributed to Boston and Sandwich Glass Co., 1830s
Clear
7¼" H.

Lacy, square pedestal base and blown font; ring knop and tin collar.

Bennington Museum

2-1 Oil Lamp
Boston and Sandwich Glass Co.
1835-40
Clear
8" H.

Circle and Ellipse pattern; blown-molded font and pressed hex-agonal base.

Robertson and Thornton Antiques Doylestown, Pa.

2-2 Fluid Lamp
Boston and Sandwich Glass Co.
1850s
Clear
12" H.

Pressed and blown-molded font; hexagonal pressed base; brass burner and collar. Horn of Plenty pattern introduced in the 1850s by the Sandwich Co. Also made by M'Kee Bros., Pittsburgh, and sold as the Comet pattern.

Bennington Museum

2-3 Oil Lamp
New England Glass Co., Cam-
    bridge, Mass., c. 1860
Clear font, milk glass base
9½" H.

Blown-molded font and pressed
base. Brass collar, brass ferrules
joining font and base, and brass
burner.

Bennington Museum

2-4 Oil Lamp
Boston and Sandwich Glass Co.
1865-70
Font with white to clear overlay;
    opaque white base
12¾" H.

Stepped, pressed base with brass
ferrules; blown-molded font with
brass collar. Widely reproduced
in the 20th century. The originals
were produced as late as the
1880s by Sandwich and other
manufacturers. Fitted for electricity.

Robertson & Thornton Antiques
Doylestown, Pa.

2-5 Oil Lamp
Boston and Sandwich Glass Co.
1860s-70s
Clear font, blue opaque base
14½" H.

Blown-molded font with cut decoration in lyre and floral motif. Pedestal base is fluted and scalloped. Brass ferrules joining font and base; brass collar. Fitted for electricity.

Bennington Museum

2-6 Oil Lamp
Ripley and Co., Pittsburgh
Patented 1870
Opaque blue fonts, clambroth
match holder and white
opaque base
15" H. to top of burner

A version of the "Bride's" or "Marriage Lamp" with blown fonts, a pressed cavity for holding matches, and a pressed base.

Bennington Museum

3 | Standard Lamps, Pressed

Few collectors can resist the colorful one-piece pressed lamps made by Sandwich and many other glassmakers in the 1840s and '50s. In form, they are very similar to the simple vases of the same period; such patterns as Four-Printie-Block and Ellipse (both 3-0) are among the first generally recognizable designs used in the glass industry. Such colors as royal purple, canary, and clambroth are also hallmarks of the period. A lamp that has been pressed in one piece has a sculpted quality to it. This is evident in such examples as 3-2 and 3-8. By comparison, the later pressed lamps, most often made in clear glass of a non-flint variety, are less dramatic. In the use of a marble base and a brass pedestal, however, the kerosene-burning fixture may give an air of solidity and luxury. Many examples of this type of lamp have been converted to electricity for use today and make imposing fixtures. The brass used for the standards, however, often has not aged very well and may need reconditioning.

Two small lamps, 3-6 and 3-7, might well be included in chapter 1. They are, however, late kerosene-burning fixtures which were clearly not intended as miniature novelties or for exclusive use in the bedchamber. They are typical of the patterned wares popular in the late Victorian period.

3-O Oil Lamp (color plate, left)
Boston and Sandwich Glass Co., c. 1840
Royal purple
10¼" H.; base, 3⅜" D.

Ellipse pattern hexagonal font with six panels; plinth base. Also made in clear, vaseline, and canary. Royal purple is very rare.

Oil Lamp (right)
Maker unknown, New England, 1840s
Canary
12" H.

Four-Printie-Block pattern font; hexagonal, flaring pedestal base.

Bennington Museum

3-1 Oil Lamp
Boston and Sandwich Glass Co.
1835-40
Clear
10" H.

Circle and Ellipse pattern font set on a monument base.

Robertson & Thornton Antiques Doylestown, Pa.

3-2 Oil Lamp
Maker unknown, 1860s
Clambroth
10⅝" H.; base, 5" D.

Flattened Sawtooth pattern font set on a hexagonal pedestal base.

Nancy Olsson Antiques Durham, Pa.

3-3 Oil Lamp
Maker unknown, 1870s
Clear
10½" H. to collar

Diamond in Ovals pattern pressed
font on brass pedestal and square
marble base. Fitted for electricity.

Bennington Museum

3-4 Oil Lamp
Maker unknown, 1870s
Clear
9¾" H. to collar

Loop pattern pressed font on
brass pedestal and square marble base. Fitted for electricity.

Bennington Museum

3-5 Oil Lamp
Boston and Sandwich Glass Co.
1850s
Clear
8½" H.

Waffle and Thumbprint pattern font on fluted standard and circular base. Also made by the New England Glass Co. and sold under the pattern name of "Palace."

Bennington Museum

3-6 Oil Lamp Base
Attributed to Boston and
    Sandwich Glass Co., 1880s
Cranberry
4" H., 3¾" D.

Inverted Heart pattern in lower half of base; variant of Bull's-Eye pattern in upper half; brass collar.

Bennington Museum

3-7 Low-Handled Oil Lamp
Maker unknown, 1870s
Clear, non-flint
3" H.

One-Hundred-One pattern base, with molded handle and brass collar.

Bennington Museum

3-8 Whale Oil Lamp
Boston and Sandwich Glass Co.
1850-60
Opaque white and grease blue
9¾" H.

Waffle pattern font in blue and plain white hexagonal base. The lamp is without its burner.

Private Collection

4 | Vases

The brilliantly colored flint glass vases produced by Sandwich in the 1840s and '50s clearly stand out as the most handsome of this decorative form. Their simplicity of line is neoclassical in inspiration; the smooth execution vividly illustrates how artfully models were prepared and then translated in the mechanical pressing process. Illustrated are many of the most popular of the patterns—Ring and Oval, Loop, Arch, Three-Printie-Block, Circle and Ellipse, Bigler, Tulip—used in the New England factories and in the Pittsburgh area as well. The colors—amethyst; electric, light, and sapphire blue; and emerald green—are representative as well. The only missing hue in this traditional rainbow is canary. The flaring or gauffered rim is typical of the form; so, too, is a hexagonal or square base. Because these vases have returned to popularity in the 20th century, they have been widely reproduced. The collector should study the pattern carefully to see if it is accurately rendered. It is unlikely, of course, that modern copies will have the weight of the flint originals. It is also possible that new glass will be too "pure" in its execution, missing slight imperfections or the small pieces of flint which often escaped the annealing process.

Vases made during the later years of the Victorian period are more extravagant in decoration and form. Both 4-7 and 4-8 are examples of transitional types which incorporate pattern-glass designs. The last example in marble glass, 4-9, illustrates how imaginative the pressing process had become in the Art Nouveau period.

4-0 Vase (color plate, left to right)
Boston and Sandwich Glass Co., c. 1840
Blue purple
9¼" H.

Ring and Oval pattern; gauffered rim, and hexagonal base. Unique color in this pattern.

Vase
Boston and Sandwich Glass Co., 1830s
Light blue
11" H.

Loop pattern; gauffered rim, hexagonal standard, and stepped base.

Vase
Boston and Sandwich Glass Co., c. 1825
Amethyst
8½" H.

Arch pattern with twelve panels; gauffered rim and square base. Extremely rare form and color. Previously thought to have been made by Stiegel at Mannheim, Pa.

Vase
Boston and Sandwich Glass Co., c. 1840

Electric blue
9 ⅞ " H.

Three-Printie-Block pattern; gauffered rim and hexagonal base. Rare color.

Bennington Museum

4-1 Vase
Boston and Sandwich Glass Co.
c. 1840
Electric Blue
7¼" H.

Circle and Ellipse pattern; gauffered rim and hexagonal base. Rare color.

Bennington Museum

4-2 Vase
Boston and Sandwich Glass Co.
c. 1840
Sapphire blue
11¾" H.

Bigler pattern; gauffered rim and square plinth base. Unusually tall for pattern and rare in color.

Bennington Museum

4-3 Vase
Boston and Sandwich Glass Co.
c. 1840
Amethyst
8⅝" H.

Arch pattern; gauffered rim and square plinth base. Unusual pattern with plinth base; rare color.

Bennington Museum

4-4 Vase
Boston and Sandwich Glass Co.
c. 1840
Deep amethyst
11⅝" H.

Arch pattern with flattened, fluted, and flared top; hexagonal base. Very rare color.

Bennington Museum

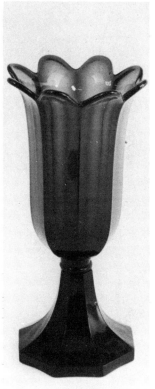

4-5 Vase
Boston and Sandwich Glass Co.
c. 1840
Deep amethyst
11½" H.

Bigler pattern; gauffered rim and square plinth base. Very rare color.

Bennington Museum

4-6 Vase
Boston and Sandwich Glass Co.
c. 1840
Emerald green
10¼" H.

Tulip pattern; paneled, gauffered rim, and octagonal bowl and base. Rare color.

Bennington Museum

4-7 Vase
Boston and Sandwich Glass Co.
c. 1850
Clear
10" H.

Tulip with Sawtooth pattern; flared hexagonal bowl, and circular base.

Frenchtown House of Antiques
Frenchtown, N.J.

4-8 Vase
Maker unknown, 1860s
Clear
10¼" H.

Waffle and Drape pattern; paneled, flared octagonal bowl, and circular base.

Bennington Museum

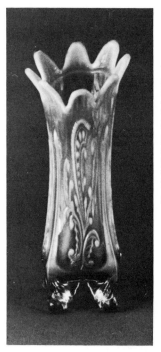

4-9 Vase
Maker unknown, Pittsburgh area
1870s-80s
Variegated green and white
8¾" H.

Fan and Feather pattern in "marble glass" or "slag glass." Challinor, Taylor & Co. produced such ware, termed "mosaic glass," in the 1870s and '80s.

Bennington Museum

5 | Candlesticks, Pressed and Blown or Blown-Molded

As with the first lamps made in the pressed glass factories, a combination of techniques was employed for the early candlesticks. The examples illustrated in this chapter draw together pressed, blown-molded, and blown elements. In most cases, the socket which holds the candle is blown, as is also the shaft. Here again, duplicating the process used with lamps, one part is joined with another by the use of wafers or knops. The example from the Pittsburgh area, 5-2, handsomely illustrates how artfully this could be achieved. The period in which such combination sticks were made was relatively short—from the 1820s to the 1840s—since it later became fairly easy to press such objects in one piece. Unlike a lamp, there was no need for a reservoir; all of the stick, in short, functioned as a base for a candle. The completely pressed candlestick is anticipated in the use of pressed sockets (middle object, 5-0 and 5-1). To find a lacy socket, however, is virtually impossible. The bases used on these sticks often duplicate those found on lamps. Such interchangeability became a feature of the American pressed glass industry.

5-O Candlestick (color plate, left to right)
Maker unknown, Pittsburgh area, 1830s
Clear
6¾" H.

Blown socket with flaring, turned-up rim; blown shaft. Hexagonal pressed base.

Candlestick
Boston and Sandwich Glass Co., c. 1830
Blue purple
9¾" H.

Lacy, pressed socket; blown, ribbed shaft with a double melon knop. Shaft rests on a stepped, pressed cloverleaf plinth. The only known example in this color.

Candlestick
Maker unknown, Pittsburgh area, 1830s
Clear
9" H.

Blown socket with flaring, turned-up rim; blown shaft with double hexagonal knop. Shaft rests on hexagonal pressed base.

Bennington Museum

5-1 Candlesticks

Boston and Sandwich Glass Co., c. 1830
Clear
9" H.

Each with pressed socket; blown, ribbed shaft with a double melon knop. Shaft rests on a stepped, pressed base fluted on the inside.

Robertson and Thornton Antiques
Doylestown, Pa.

5-2 Candlesticks
Maker unknown, Pittsburgh area, c. 1830
Clear
8¾" H.

Each with blown socket; blown shaft with a double melon knop. Shaft rests on square, stepped base.

Robertson and Thornton Antiques
Doylestown, Pa.

6 | Candlesticks, Pressed

Candlesticks pressed in one piece were produced as abundantly as lamps by the early glassmakers in the East and Midwest. Sandwich and the New England Glass Co., Cambridge, Mass., were probably responsible for the bulk of the production from the 1830s through the '50s. As with vases, the simple early designs have been especially treasured and thus have survived until the present. The Dolphin-form standard for holding a socket aloft is the most imaginative of early-Victorian pressed designs. The Petticoat Dolphin form (6-3), named for the fanciful skirt which serves as a base, dates from mid-century and was probably first introduced in the Pittsburgh area. The Crucifix form is original to Sandwich and was most often produced in opaque colors. Collectors today must be extremely wary of reproduction sticks in the Dolphin, Petticoat Dolphin, or Crucifix forms. Most of these copies, however, are not made of a flint glass and weigh noticeably less than the originals.

The ordinary type of pressed stick from the period 1830-70 is still a thing of beauty. The Petal and Loop pattern is common, with canary yellow being the most frequently encountered color. Opaque colors—so-called "grease" blue, clambroth, and a creamy white—were popular in the 1840s and '50s. Other widely produced forms are the columnar "Colonial" patterns, with simple paneled shafts and hexagonal or circular bases. Production of pressed candlesticks continued well into the 20th century; they do not begin to match, however, the work of the flint glass artists.

6-O Candlestick (color plate, left to right)
Boston and Sandwich Glass Co., c. 1840
Electric blue
10½" H.

Dolphin form with petal socket and single-step plinth base. Color is very rare in this form.

Candlestick
Boston and Sandwich Glass Co., 1840s
Canary
7" H. to brass ring socket

Triple dolphin form set on square plinth. Socket and globe are original.

Candlestick
Boston and Sandwich Glass Co., c. 1840
Clear
8½" H.

Dolphin form with Dolphin pattern socket and single-step base. Rarest of Sandwich dolphins because of impressed dolphin socket.

Candlestick
Boston and Sandwich Glass Co., c. 1840
Grease blue
10¾" H.

Dolphin form with petal socket and double-step plinth base. Extremely rare color.

Bennington Museum

6-1 Pair of Candlesticks
Boston and Sandwich Glass Co., c. 1840
Canary
6⅞" H.

Petal and Loop pattern with two hexagonal shoulders resting on a circular base.

Bennington Museum

6-2 Candlesticks
Boston and Sandwich Glass Co., 1860s
Opaque white
10" H.

Crucifix form with sloping hexagonal base. Probably made for home

as well as ecclesiastical use.

Robertson and Thornton Antiques
Doylestown, Pa.

6-3 Pair of Candlesticks
Maker unknown, Pittsburgh area, 1860s

Light blue
6¾" H.

Petticoat Dolphin form with dome-shaped base or skirt. Helen and George S. McKearin attributed this form to M'Kee Bros., Pittsburgh, but is does not appear in their catalogues of the 1860s. It might be attributed to Bakewell, Pears & Co., also of Pittsburgh.

Bennington Museum

6-4 Candlestick
Boston and Sandwich Glass Co.
1840-50
Cobalt blue
11" H.

Paneled candlestick in Colonial pattern; hexagonal base.

Private Collection

6-5 Candlestick
Boston and Sandwich Glass Co.
1860s
Clear
6½" H.

Petal socket, ribbed stem, and Diamond Point pattern base.

Bennington Museum

7 | Spill Holders

Spill holders are a form representative of a time when the lighting of lamps and fires was a daily household task. Matches were expensive to use in the first half of the 19th century and "spills," long tapers of twisted paper often feathered at the end, were a practical alternative. A holder for them in pressed glass might be kept on the mantel or next to a whale oil table lamp. The design used to decorate the piece often matched the pattern found in the lamp bowl. Illustrated here, among others, are such patterns as Harp or Lyre, Prism and Flattened Sawtooth, Quilted Diamond, Arched Band and Prism, Horn of Plenty, and a variant of Excelsior. The stained Vine design which appears in the color illustration, 7-0, illustrates the trend toward naturalistic decoration which was occurring in the late 1850s and '60s. In addition to their use as holders of spills, these objects were advertised by their makers and used in the home for holding cigars.

The usual form of a spill holder is hexagonal or round. The stems are short and the rims, sometimes banded, are smooth. These holders are not to be confused with spoon holders (see chapter 39), a somewhat later form with a longer stem, deeper bowl, and an irregular or scalloped rim. Use of glass spill holders gradually diminished in the 1860s and '70s, their place being taken by tin and silver-plated match safes.

7-O Spill Holder (color plate)
Boston and Sandwich Glass Co., 1850s
Clear, stained in two shades of green
4½" H.

Vine pattern with stained decoration and gilt rim. The same pattern is also found without staining in this form. Especially prized in the goblet form.

Robertson and Thornton Antiques
Doylestown, Pa.

7-1 Spill Holder
Maker unknown, 1840s-50s
Clear
5⅛" H., 3½" D.

Prism and Flattened Sawtooth pattern; circular form on hexagonal stem and circular base.

Nancy Olsson Antiques
Durham, Pa.

7-2 Spill Holder
Bryce Bros., Pittsburgh
1840s-50s
Clear
4½" H., 3" D.

Harp or Lyre pattern; hexagonal form on circular base.

Nancy Olsson Antiques
Durham, Pa.

7-3 Spill Holder
Boston and Sandwich Glass Co.
1840s-50s
Clear
4½" H., 3¼" D.

Early Quilted Diamond pattern; circular stem and base. Band of oval impressions at top.

Frenchtown House of Antiques
Frenchtown, N.J.

7-4 Spill Holder
Boston and Sandwich Glass Co.
1850s
Clear
5" H., 3" D.

Two-Way Heart pattern with diamond bands; circular stem and base.

Nancy Olsson Antiques
Durham, Pa.

7-5 Spill Holder
Maker unknown, 1850s
Clear
5" H., 3⅛" D.

Arched Band and Prism pattern; short, circular stem and base.

Nancy Olsson Antiques
Durham, Pa.

7-6 Spill Holder
Maker unknown, 1850s-60s
Clear
4¾" H., 3¼" D.

Unidentified ribbed pattern; circular stem and base.

Nancy Olsson Antiques
Durham, Pa.

7-7 Spill Holder
Maker unknown, Pittsburgh area
1860s
Clear
5⅜" H., 3⅝" D.

Variant of Excelsior pattern; twelve-sided, with hexagonal stem on circular base.

Nancy Olsson Antiques
Durham, Pa.

7-8 Spill Holder
Maker unknown, 1860s
Clear
4⅝" H., 3⅝" D.

Prism and Sawtooth pattern; octagonal form with petal rim. Circular stem and base.

Nancy Olsson Antiques
Durham, Pa.

7-9 Spill Holders
Maker unknown, Pittsburgh, 1865-75
Clear
Left to right: 4¾" H., 3¼" D.; 5⅞" H., 3¼" D.; 4½" H., 3½" D.

All in Star and Buckle pattern; hexagonal forms with circular bases.

Nancy Olsson Antiques
Durham, Pa.

7-10 Spill Holder
Boston and Sandwich Glass Co.
1850s
Clear
4½" H.

Horn of Plenty pattern; round stem and base.

Bennington Museum

8 | Furniture Knobs, Doorknobs, Pulls, and Tiebacks

The pressed glass industry in America began with the production of knobs and pulls. John Bakewell, Jr., of the Pittsburgh firm of Bakewell, Pears & Co., was the first to secure a patent on pressed knobs in 1825, and the New England firms followed suit in the next few years. The pressing method was ideally suited for the widespread manufacture of such small objects, although it would take some years before all the intricacies of production were mastered. Threaded glass shanks, for example, broke off easily. The use of pewter or cast iron bolts or stems became the rule. These were perfect for the curtain tiebacks, which were a part of household decoration in the mid-to-late 1800s. The designs used for the knobs, pulls, and tiebacks are not as easy to classify as tablewares. A majority were probably made in a floral pattern, but designs in imitation of cut glass—Diamond Point, star and diamond, swirls—were also popular. Color was employed in the production of these articles, those in fiery opalescent being among the most attractive. Some of the objects are marked by their maker, but many remain as anonymous as the majority of pressed glass pieces. Collectors of these simple but beautiful pieces always try to compare and match their finds. This isn't always possible. As one writer commented in **Antiques** in the 1920s: "Secure a single one, and, however conventional its design, you seem never able to match it exactly. You may think it easy to find a mate; but try it."

8-O Knobs and Pulls (color plate, clockwise from amber knob)
Makers unknown, Early to mid-1800s
Amber knob, 2¼" D.

Amber knob; scalloped petal pattern; threaded shank.

Blue opaque pull; ray pattern; round.

White opalescent pull; ray pattern; round.

Clear knob with bolt; star and diamond pattern; hexagonal.

Canary threaded pull; petal pattern.

Opalescent white knob with bolt; swirls pattern.

Bennington Museum

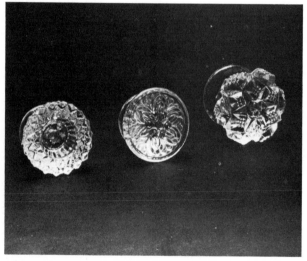

8-1 Knobs (left to right)
Makers unknown, Early to mid-1800s
Knob at far left, 2" D.

Clear; depressed center; Diamond Point pattern.

Clear; flower pattern.

Clear; star and diamond pattern.

Bennington Museum

8-2 Tiebacks (left to right)
Makers unknown, Mid-1800s
Left, 3½" D.; right, 3⅜" D.

Clear; six petals; pewter stem.

Clear; stippled petal design; pewter stem.

Bennington Museum

8-3 Tiebacks
Boston and Sandwich Glass Co., Mid-1800s
Milk Glass
4½" D.

A pair of curtain tiebacks with pewter studs.

Bennington Museum

8-4 Tiebacks
Maker unknown, Mid-1800s
Opalescent
Left, 4¼" D.; right, 5½" D.

Each with petal design and nickel-plated, cast-iron stud, and pewter nut.

Bennington Museum

 | **Window Glass**

Very little is known about the production of pressed window glass. Its use seems to have been almost purely decorative. Only small squares of glass designed for minor architectural purposes appear to have been made according to the pressing technique. Four of the best known examples, lacy panes measuring 5 x 6⅞ inches (including 9-0), were probably made in Pittsburgh in 1835-40. The example illustrated in color was used as a door panel pane in the Schenley mansion in Pittsburgh. It was once thought that similar panes were made for steamboat cabin windows. One example, produced by J. & C. Ritchie in Wheeling, West Va., is known to exist. If others were made, they have disappeared along with the Ohio River steamers. Evidently, pressed, lacy window glass was made only in the Midwest. Other examples of pressed panes, such as 9-1, may have been custom-produced by factories throughout the country in the 19th century. These were often used as side lights or transom lights. The glass used in hanging lamps was likely to be engraved or etched rather than pressed. A square of pressed glass, however, was sometimes used at the table as a tile or plate holder.

9-O Windowpane (color plate)
Maker unknown, Pittsburgh area, 1835-40
Lacy, clear
5" x 6⅞"

A door-panel pane from the Schenley mansion in Pittsburgh; possibly made by the Fort Pitt Glass Works or Bakewell, Page and Bakewell, since both firms advertised such pieces.

Bennington Museum

9-1 Windowpane
Maker unknown, New York State, 1870s
Sapphire
4" sq.

A naturalistic ivy design with a stippled background; probably used as a side light or for a transom.

Robertson and Thornton Antiques
Doylestown, Pa.

10 | Salts, Lacy

After cup plates and goblets, salt dishes have probably been the most popular objects collected by admirers of early pressed glass. The objects come in a great variety of colors and forms. Salts were among the first items widely produced by such makers as Sandwich, New England Glass, and the Jersey Glass Co. of Jersey City although they were also made in the Philadelphia and Pittsburgh areas. Lacy designs were not, however, among the very first to appear on the market. The first patterns were simpler and more regular in form; they did not depend on fine stippling for their effect. The color illustration, 10-0, shows two of the most common lacy patterns and forms—a Crown pattern scrolled salt and a Shell pattern scalloped salt. Another favorite form was the "boat" shape, illustrated in 10-2. Most salt dishes are not marked; the boat salt made by J. & T. Robinson and the Providence example, are rarities. Glass is a perfect medium for salt dishes, as other materials are easily corroded by the substance. That is why silver salts are usually provided with glass liners. Not until the late 19th century was salt generally used from a shaker.

10-0 Salt (color plate, left)
Boston and Sandwich Glass Co., 1830-40
Lacy, sapphire blue
3" L.

Crown pattern salt with star and leaf motif on sides and fleur-de-lis motif on each end. Scrolled edges and feet with scalloped apron. According to McKearin, also available in clear, opalescent, opaque white, and purple blue.

Salt (color plate, right)
Maker unknown, New England area, 1830-40
Lacy, light amethyst
2 ⅞" L.

Shell pattern salt with a shell-like ornament on each side and end. Scalloped rim and hollow base. According to McKearin, also found in clear, deep blue, light sage green, yellow green, and emerald green.

Bennington Museum

10-1 Salt
Providence Flint Glass Co., Providence, R.I., c. 1831
Lacy, clear
2¾" L.

Salt with word "PROVIDENCE" pressed on base, read correctly when looking into the vessel. Scrolled rim and footed base. According to

McKearin, also found in sapphire blue and moonstone.

Bennington Museum

10-2 Salt
J. & T. Robinson, Stourbridge Flint Glass Works, Pittsburgh, 1835
Lacy, clear
3½" L.

Boat salt with "J. Robinson & Son Pittsburgh" marked on stern and on the anchor on the bottom of the base. A seven-pointed star against a stippled field is found on each paddle wheel. Left-hand scroll on stern is missing. According to McKearin, also found in sapphire blue and deep amethyst.

Bennington Museum

11 | Salts, Solid Color

Salts not clearly designated as being lacy in execution were the first produced by the pressed glass companies. Illustration 11-1 shows one such example, a simple rectangle with a "Basket of Fruit" design and pillared corners. Equally rare is the covered, opaque blue salt in the Beaded Scroll and Basket of Flowers pattern, illustrated in color. It is not often that one can find a cover that exactly matches a dish. Only dishes with hinged covers or threaded tops, such as syrup pitchers and casters, were likely to survive intact. Because of historical associations, the "Lafayet" boat salt is also considered valuable. It is also one of the few signed Sandwich pieces. The curious spelling of the name has never been satisfactorily explained. There are a number of pressed glass objects, however, which relate to the Marquis de Lafayette's triumphal visit to the United States in 1825, and many of these date from five to ten years later.

The term "master" is used to denote a salt which stood alone or as part of a pair at the table. It was a communal rather than an individual receptacle. The individual salts, as shown in 11-6, are considerably smaller in size. Matching master and individual salts often came as part of a pattern set, as in Horn of Plenty (11-7), Ribbed Ivy (11-9), and Jacob's Ladder (11-11), from the 1850s well into the 1880s. During this period, the form of salt dishes became more and more conventional, the usual shape being a simple oval or round bowl.

11-0 Covered Salt (color plate, left to right)
Boston and Sandwich Glass Co., 1830-40
Opaque blue
3" L.

Beaded Scroll and Basket of Flowers design with pineapple finial cover. Rarely found with cover.

Salt
Attributed to Boston and Sandwich Glass Co., 1830s
Blown-molded
Opalescent
2⅛" H.

Beaded arch pattern in the Sandwich baroque style; blown-molded rather than pressed in a mold. Marked on base: "R & C A Wright Philadelphia." The firm traded in domestic and imported glassware. (See also 11-3.)

Master Salt
Boston and Sandwich Glass Co., c. 1850
Deep amethyst
3" H.

Paneled, footed master salt in hexagonal form. Rare color.

Salt
Boston and Sandwich Glass Co., c. 1830
Opaque, light blue
3½" L.

Boat salt marked "LAFAYET" on paddle wheels, "SANDWICH" on hollow bottom, and "B. & S. GLASS CO" on stern. According to McKearin, there are two other variants, one with a beaded ornament, and the other with a scroll ornament on the base rather than "SANDWICH." Known also in opalescent, opaque white, canary, and purple blue.

Bennington Museum

11-1 Salt
New England Glass Co., Cambridge, Mass., c. 1830
Opalescent
3" L.

Rectangular, footed salt with the Basket of Fruit design on sides; marked "N E GLASS COMPANY BOSTON" on base.

Bennington Museum

11-2 Salt

Jersey Glass Co., Jersey City, N.J., c. 1830
Sea green
3" L.

Rectangular, footed salt with Basket of Flowers design on both sides; marked on base "JERSEY GLASS CO. NR. [near] NEW YORK."

Bennington Museum

11-3 Salt (left)
Boston and Sandwich Glass Co., 1830s
Clear
2⅛" L.

Footed bowl and base in the Beaded Arch pattern, indicative of the Sandwich baroque style (see 11-0). Similarly decorated bowls with handles were termed "baskets."

Salt (right)
Attributed to Boston and Sandwich Glass Co., 1830s
Blown-molded
Clear
2" L.

Identical to 11-0, second from left, in decoration and marking.

Robertson and Thornton Antiques
Doylestown, Pa.

11-4 Salt
Boston and Sandwich Glass Co., 1830s
Amber
3¼" L.

Rectangular form, semi-lacy salt with serrated rim.

Robertson and Thornton Antiques
Doylestown, Pa.

11-5 Master Salt
Pittsburgh or New England area,
**   Mid-1800s**
Sapphire blue
2½" H.

Colonial pattern footed salt on octagonal base; scalloped rim.
Thought to be one of the earliest
pressed glass patterns.

Robertson and Thornton Antiques
Doylestown, Pa.

11-6 Pair of Salts
Boston and Sandwich Glass Co., 1850s-60s

Clear
2" D.

Individual salts in Cable pattern, first produced by Sandwich in commemoration of the laying of the transatlantic cable in the 1850s.

Robertson and Thornton Antiques
Doylestown, Pa.

11-7 Salt
Possibly Boston and Sandwich Glass Co., 1850s
Clear
3¼" W.

Oval salt in Horn of Plenty pattern. The same pattern is known to have been produced by M'Kee Bros., Pittsburgh, and was named "Comet."

Bennington Museum

11-8 Pair of Salts
Maker unknown, Mid-1800s
Clear

2½" H., 3" D.

Round, footed salts in Flattened Sawtooth pattern. Ruth Webb Lee explains how this pattern differs from the regular Sawtooth pattern: "Instead of a sharp-pointed apex to the diamond, it is truncated, the flattened end looking as though a knife had cut off the point." Made by at least several factories.

Frenchtown House of Antiques
Frenchtown, N.J.

11-9 Master Salt
Boston and Sandwich Glass Co., 1850s
Clear
2¾" H., 2¾" D.

Footed salt in Ribbed Ivy pattern. According to Ruth Webb Lee, a number of forms were produced in this popular pattern.

Bennington Museum

11-10 Pair of Master Salts
Maker unknown, Mid-1800s
"Vaseline" yellow
3½" D.

Flat Diamond pattern in imitation of cut glass.

Bennington Museum

11-11 Pair of Master Salts
Bryce Bros., Pittsburgh, 1880s
Clear, non-flint
2¾" H., 2¾" D.

Footed salts in Jacob's Ladder or Maltese pattern. Jagged rim, faceted stem, and clear base. The original trade name was "Maltese."

Frenchtown House of Antiques
Frenchtown, N.J.

**11-12 Covered Master Salt
New England or Pittsburgh areas,
    Mid-1800s
Clear
5¼" H.**

Sawtooth pattern covered salt
with hexagonal stem tapering to
circular base.

Frenchtown House of Antiques
Frenchtown, N.J.

12 | Cup Plates, Historical Designs

Cup plates can be studied endlessly, as Ruth Webb Lee and James H.
Rose proved so effectively in **American Glass Cup Plates**, published
in 1948. Over 1,000 designs have been chronicled to date and it is
clear that nearly every 19th-century pressed glass factory active between the 1830s and '60s produced such items. Since they only cost
around five cents each, their use was almost unlimited. It is said that
1,600 a day could be turned out by a man and his apprentice. Ranging from approximately three inches in diameter to four inches, these
were among the easiest of articles to press. This did not necessarily
make them any less attractive to the eye. Some carry portraits, others
historical scenes; the majority are impressed with geometric or floral
designs.

These were not plates that were simply slipped under a cup to
catch the overflow. Cup plates were actually used to drink from. The
custom until the mid-19th century was to serve hot tea in a cup and
then to pour it into the saucer or plate to cool before drinking. The
plate, then, was a more important surface to decorate than the cup.

Most discussions of cup plates divide the subject into two
categories of design—historical and conventional. The latter type,

however, is neither descriptive nor especially useful. For our purposes, the subject has been divided into three categories: historical designs, geometric designs, and representational designs. Many of the historical plates feature portrait busts of noteworthy figures from the 1830s—Henry Clay, Victoria and Albert, Robert Livingston, William Henry Harrison—and are relatively easy to date. Also simple to pinpoint in time are the commemorative plates such as 12-5. The Fort Pitt American eagle plate is included here (12-2) because it is essentially historical or patriotic, as is the Log Cabin pattern plate (12-7), the Cadmus (12-8), the bald eagle (12-9), and the plow plate (12-10).

These historical designs were not among the first produced. Sandwich was making cup plates as early as 1827; the Pittsburgh glassmakers began at roughly the same time, if not earlier. As with salt dishes, the first designs were simple and not stippled in the lacy mode. Lacy plates, including many of the historical designs, became popular in the 1830s.

References to the Lee and Rose work on cup plates are included in many of the entries. This should make it easier for the reader to seek additional information on various sizes and types of decoration (stippling, rim design, shoulder patterns, etc.). To lose one's place in this essential, but poorly printed book, is to invite almost instant madness.

12-0 Cup Plate (color plate, left to right)
Boston and Sandwich Glass Co., 1840s
Clear
3½" D.

Henry Clay portrait bust, facing left. Four shields in border and even serrations in rim; "HENRY CLAY" with star below bust. Perhaps made at the time of Clay's 1844 presidential campaign.

Cup Plate
Boston and Sandwich Glass Co., c. 1840
Lacy, clear
4¼" D.

Toddy-sized plate with Victoria and Albert portrait busts. Made to celebrate the royal wedding in 1840; rose, thistle, and shamrock in border symbolize the United Kingdom. "VICTORIA & ALBERT" above busts.

Cup Plate
Boston and Sandwich Glass Co., c. 1830
Lacy, clear
3½" D.

Chancellor Livingston steamboat cup plate. Border of scrolls, stars, shields, and hearts. Border hearts are not stippled in this version. The ship, beginning in the late 1820s, traveled between Providence and New York and was named for Robert Livingston. "CHANCELLOR" is pressed above the ship and "LIVINGSTON" below.

Bennington Museum

12-1 Cup Plate
Boston and Sandwich Glass Co., 1830s
Lacy border, amber center

3½" D.

Identical in almost every way to the previous example, except for its amber stain in the center.

Bennington Museum

12-2 Cup Plate

Fort Pitt Glass Works, Pittsburgh, 1835
Lacy, clear
3¾" D.

An American eagle in the so-called "Fort Pitt" cup-plate design. The border is of the Peacock Feather pattern; "FORT PITT" is impressed on a scroll borne by the eagle. Twenty-four stars—symbolizing the states—appear in the background.

Bennington Museum

12-3 Cup Plate
Boston and Sandwich Glass Co., c. 1840
Lacy, clear
3⅞" D.

Identical in every way—except size—to the example illustrated in color (12-0), which approximates a toddy-sized cup plate. This example, however, is much closer to the standard size.

Bennington Museum

12-4 Cup Plate
Boston and Sandwich Glass Co., 1841
Clear

3¼' D.

William Henry Harrison portrait bust, with twenty-six stars and legends "MAJ. GEN. W. H. HARRISON" and "BORN.FEB.9.1773." in center. Draped border with legends "PRESIDENT" above and "1841" below. Elected to the presidency in 1840, Harrison died a year later.

Bennington Museum

12-5 Cup Plate

Boston and Sandwich Glass Co., c. 1843
Clear
3½" D.

Bunker Hill cup plate, probably made in the year the monument was dedicated. The legend in the outer border reads "CORNERSTONE LAID BY LAFAYETTE. JUNE. 17. 1825" above, and "FINISHED BY THE LADIES. 1841" below. Ruth Webb Lee speculates that these plates were sold as souvenirs. The legend in the inner border reads: "BUNKER HILL BATTLE FOUGHT JUNE 17 1775" and "FROM THE FAIR TO THE BRAVE."

Frenchtown House of Antiques
Frenchtown, N.J.

12-6 Cup Plate
Attributed to Boston and Sandwich Glass Co., c. 1832
Lacy, clear
3⅜" D.

Henry Clay portrait bust, facing right. Stippled border with fleur-de-lis; center contains legend "HENRY.CLAY" and sprays of laurel at right, oak and acorns at left. Most experts believe this design to be older than that already illustrated in color (12-0), and is most definitely much rarer. The plate may have been issued earlier during Clay's 1832 presidential campaign.

Bennington Museum

12-7 Cup Plate
Probably Boston and Sandwich Glass Co., c. 1840-41
Clear

3¼" D.

Log Cabin pattern plate, made during or soon after the presidential campaign of William Henry Harrison, the so-called "Log Cabin and Hard Cider Candidate." Both of these elements are represented on the plate. Probably Lee No. 594. The rim is made up of sixty-six even scallops.

Bennington Museum

12-8 Cup Plate

Probably Boston and Sandwich Glass Co., c. 1824-30
Clear
3½" D.

The Cadmus pattern, illustrating the ship on which the Marquis de Lafayette traveled to America on his triumphal trip in 1824. Due to the plate's condition, it is impossible to determine which of several Lee examples (No. 610-A, B, C, or D) matches this. The versions differ in the number of scallops in the rim.

Bennington Museum

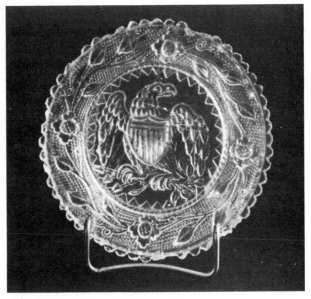

12-9 Cup Plate
Probably midwestern, Mid-1800s
Lacy, clear
3" D.

Central design of American bald eagle with sawtooth border encircling it. The rim consists of fifty-six even scallops. According to Lee (No. 668), also known in a bold pink tint.

Bennington Museum

12-10 Cup Plate
Probably Pittsburgh, 1840-41
Lacy, clear
3¼" D.

Plow pattern, another of the artifacts of the campaign and short-lived administration of William Henry Harrison. This design differs from several others in that the plow handles are joined by a crossbar. This version also contains more foliage than the others. (See Lee No. 687, 688, 689). There are twenty-four bull's-eyes in the rim with a point between each.

Bennington Museum

13 | Cup Plates, Geometric Designs

Most of the geometric pattern cup plates date from the 1830s and '40s. A surprising number of them were produced in color, although examples in clear predominate. The earliest plates (13-6 and 13-7) from the 1820s were probably made in clear glass only. The designs on both these early plates and many of the later ones were borrowed from the cut glass tradition. The Roman Rosette design (13-0, back row, right); the fleur-de-lis and diamond design shown in 13-3; and the star, diamond and rosettes example, 13-7, were inspired by work in cut glass.

In comparing one plate to another, it is important to take note of the rim or edge design. Is it smooth or serrated? Is it made up of scallops, points, or both? Are the rims smooth or ragged? There are subtle differences in cup plates made in New England, Philadelphia, and the Pittsburgh area which will defy the amateur's eye. Early cup plates, like other pieces of a similar age, are likely to be heavier in weight than the later. The thickness of glass may be almost double. Early pieces may also exhibit more surface imperfections, such as fissures or bubbles. Despite these apparent blemishes, these imperfect plates are often much more brilliant than later examples.

Unless one intends to concentrate on collecting only later pattern glass, a study of cup plates can be especially rewarding. Because of the vast number of patterns pressed (more than in any other form), one is introduced to almost the full repertory of the early glassmaker.

13-O Cup Plate (color plate, back row, left to right)
New England area, probably Boston and Sandwich Glass Co.
Mid-1800s
Honey amber
3⅛" D.

Rosette design (Lee, No. 324), paneled shoulder, and rim with sixty-six even scallops.

Cup Plate
Midwest/Pittsburgh area, or Philadelphia, 1830-45
Blue green
3⁹⁄₁₆" D.

Roman Rosette design; rim with eight large scallops and points between. According to Lee (No. 253), this is a scarce color. Also available in clear, cloudy, olive green, opalescent, and light green.

Cup Plate (front row, left to right)
Possibly Midwest, 1830-45
Lacy, dark blue
3¼" D.

Scrolled pattern surrounds central dot; sixty-six even scallops form rim. According to Lee (No. 262), also available in clear, gray blue, lavender, and amethyst; dark blue is considered scarce. A less common version can be found without the dot in the center.

Cup Plate
Possibly Boston and Sandwich Glass Co., 1835-40
Lacy, light green
3½" D.

Sunburst pattern with sixteen rays and twenty-four scallops with points between on rim. According to Lee (No. 279), also found in clear, milky, and lavender; light green is considered "plentiful."

Cup Plate
Possibly Boston and Sandwich Glass Co., 1830-45
Light blue
3½" D.

Sunburst pattern in center; star and palmette patterns in shoulder. Rim consists of fifty-nine even scallops. According to Lee (No. 333), the design is also found in clear; light blue is considered "scarce."

Bennington Museum

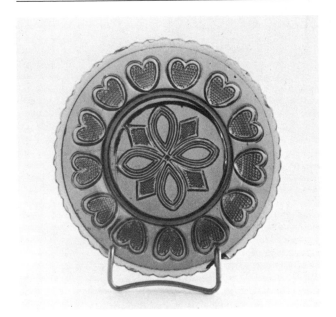

13-1 Cup Plate
Probably Boston and Sandwich Glass Co., 1835-50
Blue
3½" D.

Thirteen-Hearts in Border pattern with geometric motif in center. Rim is made up of fifty-two even scallops. Lee (No. 465-K), calls the color rare; also available in clear.

Bennington Museum

13-2 Cup Plate
Possibly New England Glass Co.,
**   Cambridge, Mass., 1829-30**
Opalescent
3⅝" D.

Eight-Hearts pattern in center with surrounding leafy motif; wheat motif in shoulder. The rim is a simple Rope pattern. Lee considers opalescent very rare in this pattern (No. 80).

Bennington Museum

13-3 Cup Plate
Philadelphia area, c. 1830
Lacy, clear
3⅜" D.

Fleur-de-lis and geometric center design; thirty-seven bull's-eyes and diamonds in shoulder. Plain rim. Lee pattern No. 107 is considered rare.

Frenchtown House of Antiques
Frenchtown, N.J.

13-4 Cup Plate
Probably Midwestern, c. 1830-45
Lacy, blue
4" D.

Unidentified geometric pattern with rim of thirty even scallops.

Ren's Antiques
Newtown, Pa.

13-5 Cup Plate
Probably Boston and Sandwich Glass Co., c. 1830-45
Lacy, slightly opalescent
3⅝" D.

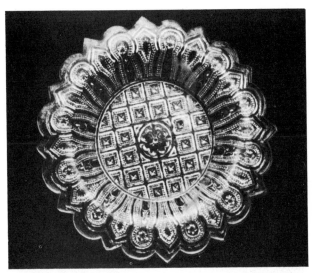

Geometric design in center with Hairpin pattern shoulder. Rim consists of twelve scallops and twelve points. According to Lee, one of the most popular Lacy patterns for cup plates. Also available in clear and completely opalescent (No. 285).

Bennington Museum

13-6 Cup Plate

New England area, or Pennsylvania, 1820s
Clear
3¾" D.

Star in center, surrounded by radiating strawberry diamond pattern and sheafs on shoulder. Rim consists of fifteen scallops with points between. According to Lee (No. 48), only made in clear; supply is considered plentiful.

Bennington Museum

13-7 Cup Plate
Boston and Sandwich Glass Co., or New England Glass Co., 1820s
Lacy, clear
3¼" D.

Star, diamond, and rosettes in center; stippled inner border. Outer border features sheafs of wheat with seven stalks, each of which is pointed. Lee identifies this plate as being available only in clear, and rates it as rare (No. 35). Rim is made up of seventeen even scallops.

Bennington Museum

13-8 Cup Plate
Probably Boston and Sandwich Glass Co., Mid-1800s
Light amethyst
3¼" D.

Star or rosette center motif and blazes in border; sixty-six even scallops

form the rim. Also available in clear, honey amber, deep amethyst, and opal. Lee No. 324.

Bennington Museum

13-9 Cup Plate
Origin unknown, 1830-45

Clear
3⅛" D.

Center boss motif; plain shoulder. Rim is made up of ninety-six even scallops. Lee No. 339. Also known to exist in light blue.

Bennington Museum

14 | Cup Plates, Representational Designs

Cup plates with floral or representational designs are found almost as often as the geometric designs. Many of them, however, were made at a later date than the abstract patterns—in the 1840s and '50s—when the fashion for cup plates was beginning to decline. Nearly all of the examples illustrated in this chapter are of the lacy variety. The fine stippling provides an effective background for the bold and familiar designs—floral motifs such as roses, pansies, and thistles; entwined and single hearts; and representations of a riverboat, a dog, and a butterfly. In general, these later cup plates are not as heavy in weight as the earlier types featuring more elaborate lacy designs. The later product from Sandwich or other factories, nevertheless, may be more finely pressed.

Reproductions of the more familiar patterns, such as the butterfly (14-2) and the hound (14-0), have been made since at least the early 1900s. As Ruth Webb Lee notes in the case of the butterfly, the perpetrator of the fraud chose colors which were clearly not antique vintage. The representational designs are easiest to copy, but the collector can often detect differences in stippling, placement of the design, and in the make-up of the elements in the rim.

14-0 Cup Plate (color plate, left to right)
Origin unknown, Mid-1800s
Clear
3¼" D.

The Hound pattern, one of the rarest and most charming of cup-plate designs. The rim has twenty-seven scallops with points between. Lee (No. 699) states that there are also plates with a pink tint, and in yellow. The hound or whippet was a favorite decorative motif in the 1840s and '50s and was often shown at the side of the figure of Prince Albert, a devotee of the sporting dog.

Cup Plate
Midwestern, 1830-45
Lacy, clear
3" D.

Rose and Pansy pattern with a rim made up of thirty bull's-eyes. Lee (No. 148) claims that it was made only in clear.

Cup Plate
Probably Boston and Sandwich Glass Co., Mid-1800s

Lacy, clear
3¼" D.

Hearts pattern, four in center and twelve in border. Rim is made up of sixty-six even scallops. According to Lee (No. 477), this pattern was also available in opalescence; clear is considered common.

Bennington Museum

14-1 Cup Plate
Midwestern, 1830-45
Lacy, clear
3¼" D.

Torch pattern; also known as "Liberty Torch" and "Victory Torch." The rim is termed a ten-scallop rope. Lee's numbering is incorrect for this version; it is shown as No. 158 and is actually No. 158-A. Clear only.

Bennington Museum

14-2 Cup Plate
Probably Boston and Sandwich Glass Co., 1830-45
Lacy, clear
3¼" D.

Butterfly pattern with stippled background; sixty-six even scallops in rim. Lee (No. 331) warns of modern reproductions, and points out that

the original plates are subtly different. There is one flower in lower right shoulder which has seven petals, rather than the six which appear in the reproductions. Only clear is known to have been produced; reproductions exist in blue and a pink amber.

Bennington Museum

14-3 Cup Plate

Probably Boston and Sandwich Glass Co., 1829-30
Lacy, deep blue
3¼" D.

Valentine pattern with four harps in shoulder. Rim is made up of twenty-four large scallops with two smaller ones filling in between. The piece illustrated is in poor condition, having lost some of the serrated edge. Lee (No. 440-B) mentions that clear, light blue, gray blue, opalescence, amethyst, and pink tint were also available.

Bennington Museum

14-4 Cup Plate
Probably Pittsburgh area, 1830s
Lacy, clear
3½" D.

Paddle Wheeler pattern in octagonal form; only a few circular examples have been found. Each of the eight sections of the rim contains seven scallops. Known only in clear. Lee No. 612-A. This plate has also been identified as "The Robert Fulton."

Bennington Museum

14-5 Cup Plate
Probably Pittsburgh area, 1830-45
Lacy, light green tint to clear

3⅜" D.

River Boat medallion pattern within grapevine frame; hairpin shoulder. The rim is made up of twenty-five scallops with a point between each. The color appears to be unique. Lee states (No. 615-A) that a clear and a pink-tint variety are known to have been made.

Bennington Museum

14-6 Cup Plate
Origin unknown, Mid-1800s
Lacy, green

4" D.

A rose and thistle design appears in the center section with a floral motif entwined in the shoulder. The rim is made up of twenty-four scallops and a point between each.

Ren's Antiques
Newtown, Pa.

15 | Entrée Dishes

The term "entrée," of fairly modern usage, has been chosen in this book to designate those serving bowls or dishes which can be used for vegetables or some other side dish at the table. A covered dish of this type might also contain a hot main course. The smallest of the dishes illustrated is 6¾ inches and the largest, 10½ inches long. Some are as deep as approximately 3½ inches and others as shallow as the lacy plate, 15-1, a mere inch or so. Entrée dishes as such were not offered by the early pressed glass manufacturers; rather, they advertised bowls and serving "plates" of varying sizes—from 6 inches to 10 inches. Even the later pattern-glass makers rarely offered a vegetable dish. Instead, as the century advanced, there was a gradual increase in specialty dishes—berry dishes, nappies in varying sizes for all varieties of food, and low-footed compotes or comports for fruit.

15-O Entrée Dish (color plate, left to right)
George Duncan and Sons, Pittsburgh, 1870s
Clear
8" L.

Oval bowl in Tree of Life pattern, Pittsburgh variety. This pattern is distinguished from that made by the Portland Glass Co. at an earlier date by the melon ribbing on each end. The clear panels are decorated with a Drape and Tassel design; a star is impressed in the base.

Entrée Dish
Boston and Sandwich Glass Co., 1839-40
Lacy, clear
8" W.

The "Pipes of Pan" motif is found in the center of this octagonal, paneled piece. The design is derived from 18th-century French crystal.

Entrée Dish
Maker unknown, 1880-1900
Amber, non-flint
2¾" H., 6½" W., 9⅞" L.

Cradle-shaped dish in Button and Daisy pattern. Besides being used for serving side courses, this may have been used as a berry bowl.

Bennington Museum

15-1 Entrée Dish
Boston and Sandwich Glass Co., 1850s
Clear
2" H., 7" W., 10" L.

Ray pattern plate with crossed Peacock Feather and Medallion design on shoulder extending to scrolled rope rim.

Bennington Museum

15-2 Entrée/Vegetable Dish
 Boston and Sandwich Glass Co., or M'Kee and Bros., Pittsburgh
 1850s
 Clear

9" L.

Crossed Peacock Feather and Medallion pattern vegetable or entrée dish; rayed center. Advertisied in 1860s M'Kee catalogues as Ray pattern dish.

Frenchtown House of Antiques
Frenchtown, N.J.

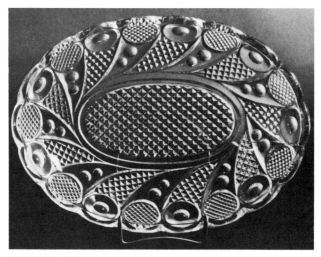

15-3 Entrée Dish
Boston and Sandwich Glass Co., 1850s
Clear
2" H., 7" W., 10" L.

Horn of Plenty oval dish, perhaps also used as a relish. The same oval form was used for making a compote with the addition of a pedestal. (See 24-12.)

Bennington Museum

15-4 Entrée/Vegetable Dish
Boston and Sandwich Glass Co., 1830s
Lacy, clear
10½" L.

Princess Feather Medallion pattern in early lacy glass; this is not to be confused with later Bakewell, Pears & Co. pattern of the 1870s with a

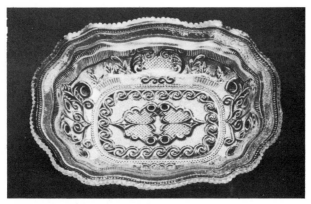

similar name. The earlier ware is heavier and more brilliant.

Bennington Museum

15-5 Covered Entrée Dish
M'Kee and Bros., Pittsburgh, 1890s
Milk glass, non-flint
4¼" H., 6¾" L.

"Dewey" pattern covered dish honoring George Dewey, admiral and hero of Manila Bay in 1898.

Bennington Museum

15-6 Entrée Dish
M'Kee and Brothers, Pittsburgh
1871

Clear
9" L.

Rustic pattern dish, available in
three sizes: 7", 8", and 9". Gillinder and Sons, Philadelphia, also
produced tableware with the pattern name of Rustic, but at a later
time and in a very different design. This dish and eighteen other
forms in Rustic are illustrated in the
1871 catalogue.

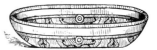

16 | Animal-Form Dishes

Dishes in the form of animals are among the most delightful of Victorian pressed glass objects. Although made largely for their novelty
value, they are not without a degree of usefulness. The Westmoreland
Specialty Co. of Grapeville, Pa., made many thousands of five-inch
hen dishes in which prepared mustard was sold. Other dishes were
used as candy containers or for serving relish. Among the manufacturers who featured animal dishes are M'Kee and Brothers and the
United States Glass Co., both of Pittsburgh; Challinor, Taylor & Co., of
Tarentum, Pa.; the Central Glass Co. of Wheeling, West Va.; and the
Sandwich company. The hen was the most popular form, but ducks,
turkeys, roosters, fish, rabbits, dogs, swans, and owls were also
honored in this manner. The earliest of these pieces are likely to be
found in opaque glass, usually white, and with glass eyes; the later
pieces may be clear (crystal) or frosted, with features emphasized
with paint. Almost all of the animal-form dishes are of a non-flint glass.

16-0 Covered Dishes and Salts (color plate)
Cambridge Glass Co., Cambridge, Ohio, Early 1900s
Frosted glass, non-flint
Heights: 9", 7", 3", 3"

Dishes in the form of turkeys, the most American of birds, were used as
candy dishes; the smaller versions as salts.

Bennington Museum

16-1 Relish Dish or Platter
Atterbury & Co., Pittsburgh, Patented 1872
Clear, non-flint
9½" L.

Double-fish design. These dishes were also produced in opalescent, white, and turquoise blue. The Atterbury firm was best known for its "duck" covered dish.

Ren's Antiques
Newtown, Pa.

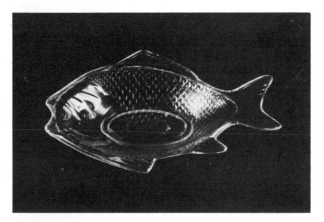

16-2 Relish Dish
Possibly Atterbury & Co., Pittsburgh
Clear, non-flint
9" L.

Single-fish design; available in same colors as in double pattern (see 16-1).

Bennington Museum

16-3 Candy Dish
Probably Cambridge Glass Co., Early 1900s
Frosted glass, non-flint
7" H.

Identical turkey form as that illustrated in 16-0.

Ren's Antiques
Newtown, Pa.

16-4 Candy Dish
Maker unknown, 1890-1910
Clear, non-flint
7" H.

A rooster with a red coxscomb and waddle is pressed in a similar way to the turkeys.

Ren's Antiques
Newtown, Pa.

16-5 Hen Dish
Pittsburgh area, 1880s-90s
Frosted glass, non-flint
5¾" H. to top of tail; 7¼" at widest point

Basket Weave pattern dish and finely pressed top; rim of dish is scalloped. Challinor, Taylor & Co. of Pittsburgh was the leading late-19th-century manufacturer of similar pieces, which continued to be produced after the merger with the U.S. Glass Co. The form of this

piece, however, differs from the typical Challinor, Taylor object.

Private Collection

17 | Sauce, Relish, Honey, and Cheese Dishes

Sauce dishes are probably the most common of pressed glass tablewares from the 19th century. Although meant for serving sauces, such objects were often used from early in the 1800s for other purposes as well. The average size is four inches in diameter, but many pattern sets include dishes in other sizes up to nearly seven inches in diameter. Illustrated here are flat sauce dishes, not the stemmed and footed variety which are featured in the next chapter. Flat dishes, which often appear to be nothing more than saucers that are slightly deeper than usual, were popular in the first half of the century. Illustrated are both lacy and plain dishes from the 1830-60 period in the Inverted Heart (17-0), Roman Rosette (17-0, Morning Glory (17-6), Rayed Peacock Feather (17-8), Horn of Plenty (17-7 and 17-12), and Flute (17-3) patterns. The most famous of the early sauce dishes is the "Industry" bowl (17-10), the story of which is told in the text accompanying the illustration. Most of these dishes are made of a heavy flint glass.

Often similar in design to later sauce dishes (from the 1860 to 1900 period) are relish, honey, and cheese dishes. Each of these varying forms filled a definite need on the late-Victorian dining table. Earlier in the century, it seems that only the honey dish (as in 17-16) was singled out for special treatment, and then only in rare instances. In contrast, Adams & Co. of Pittsburgh offered both round and square sauce dishes, a footed sauce in the Wildflower pattern of the 1870s, an oblong relish (17-3), square fruit bowls in six-inch, seven-inch, and eight-inch sizes, and other kinds of special serving dishes. Among the most popular late-Victorian patterns shown here in relish, cheese, and sauce dishes are Bird of Paradise (17-0), Daisy and Button (17-1), Good Luck (17-2 and 17-9), Diamond Quilted (17-4), and Hobnail (17-15. The cheese dishes are the only ones that are covered. Although they approximate butter dishes in form, and, indeed, may have been used interchangeably, they are included here because of their special function and limited manufacture.

17-O Sauce Dish (color plate, foreground, left to right)
Attributed to Boston and Sandwich Glass Co., Mid-1800s
Clear
3¾" D.

Inverted Heart pattern on shoulder, with scalloped rim. Pattern found also on honey dishes and bowls.

Relish
Boston and Sandwich Glass Co., 1830-45
Lacy, clear
8" L.

Double Leaf pattern, one commonly found in sauce dishes of the lacy Sandwich type. Available also in various colors.

Sauce (background, left to right)
Boston and Sandwich Glass Co., c. 1830
Lacy, dark sapphire blue
6¼" D.

This piece combines two of the most popular lacy Sandwich sauce patterns—Crossed Swords in the center and Princess Feather Medallion on the shoulder.

Cheese Dish
Northwood Glass Col, Martins Ferry, Ohio, 1880s
Iridescent, non-flint
7½" H. to top of finial

Bird of Paradise pattern covered dish with a flower finial.

Sauce
Boston and Sandwich Glass Co., c. 1845
Amethyst
5¼" D.

Roman Rosette pattern which is, according to Lee, the most common pattern used for sauce dishes by New England glassmakers. Because of its size, it might also be termed a nappy.

Bennington Museum

17-1 Relish
Maker unknown, 1880s
Amber, non-flint

1⅝" H., 3" W., 7⅞ L.

Boat-shaped dish in Daisy and Button pattern; paneled, with scalloped rim.

Bennington Museum

17-2 Relish
Probably Adams & Co., Pittsburgh, 1880s
Clear, non-flint
9" L. from handle to handle

Horseshoe or Good Luck pattern; available only in clear. Copied by other glassmakers of the period.

Bennington Museum

17-3 Relish
Adams & Co., Pittsburgh, 1870s
Canary, non-flint
1⅜" H., 4¼" W., 9⅜" L.

Wildflower pattern glass relish dish easily mistaken for a later form of butter dish. Also found in amber, blue, and clear.

Bennington Museum

17-4 Sauce
Maker unknown, 1880s
Shaded glass, non-flint
4½" D.

Diamond Quilted pattern in shaded or amberina glass. This pattern was commonly found in amberina. The Diamond Quilted pattern was originally known as Venetian Diamond. (See also 43-0 and 44-0.)

Bennington Museum

17-5 Sauce
Maker unknown, 1870s
Amber, non-flint
4" D.

Raised hexagon and diamond pattern; scalloped edge.

Bennington Museum

17-6 Sauce
Boston and Sandwich Glass Co., 1860s
Clear
4" D.

Morning Glory pattern, popular in the 1860s when introduced, and for many years thereafter. Reproduced in 20th century.

Bennington Museum

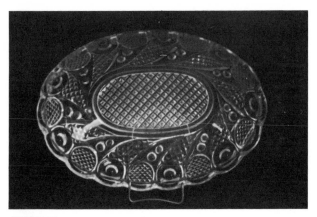

17-7 Sauce
Boston and Sandwich Glass Co., 1850s
Clear
4⁷/₁₆" D.

Oval dish in Horn of Plenty pattern; one of a set of four, with plain, scalloped edge. Colors in this pattern are rare.

Bennington Museum

17-8 Sauce
Boston and Sandwich Glass Co., 1830-45
Lacy, clear
1⅜" H., 4⅝" D.

Ray pattern and crossed Peacock Feather in shoulder; this pattern is sometimes termed "Rayed Peacock Feather" by Lee. Scalloped rim.

Bennington Museum

17-9 Sauce
Probably Adams & Co., Pittsburgh, 1880s
Clear, non-flint
4¼" D.

Horseshoe or Good Luck pattern with anchor ornament.

Bennington Museum

17-10 Sauce
Boston and Sandwich Glass Co., c. 1840
Lacy, clear
6½" D.

Like the Log Cabin cup plates and heads of William Henry Harrison (12-4 and 14-4), this dish or bowl is said to commemorate the 1840 presidential campaign. It is known as the "Industry" bowl because of the representations of manufacturing, shipping, and farming on the stippled shoulder. Examples without stippling in the shoulder are also known. This example has a scalloped rim; a plain rim type also exists.

Bennington Museum

17-11 Sauce
Boston and Sandwich Glass Co.
c. 1830
Lacy, dark blue green
4¼" D.

Identical, except in size, to dish illustrated in color plate 17-0.

Bennington Museum

17-12 Sauce
Boston and Sandwich Glass Co., 1850s
Clear
5" D.

Round sauce in Horn of Plenty pattern (in contrast to oval, 17-7); scalloped edge.

Bennington Museum

17-13 Sauce
Midwestern, 1830s
Honey amber
6⅛" D.

Flute pattern with starburst or rayed center and scalloped rim.

Robertson and Thornton Antiques
Doylestown, Pa.

17-14 Sauce
Boston and Sandwich Glass Co., 1830-45

Lacy, clear
4¼" D.

Peacock Eye border with Scrolled Eye center base. Two of the most common lacy Sandwich designs brought together, as they were on salts, compotes, and six-inch plates.

Frenchtown House of Antiques
Frenchtown, N.J.

17-15 Sauce
Maker unknown, 1880s
Blue opalescent, non-flint
3¼" D.

Hobnail pattern with what Lee terms a "frilled" or "ribbon-top" edge. Also available in a yellow hue.

Bennington Museum

17-16 Honey Dish and Tray
Boston and Sandwich Glass Co., 1830s

Lacy, clear
Dish, 6¾" L.; Tray, 7" L.

Gothic Arch pattern dish, with arches repeated on inside of cover. Tray is decorated with alternating hearts and stars.

Bennington Museum

17-17 Bonbon Dish
Attributed to Northwood Glass Co., Elwood, Pa., 1890s
Clear with ruby flashing, crystal
5¼" H., base, 5" D.

Royal Oak pattern covered dish with flashing that fades to clear at top; acorn finial.

Bennington Museum

17-18 Cheese or Butter Dish
Pittsburgh area, 1880s-90s
Clear, ruby-stained, non-flint
Base, 8" D.

A diamond pattern appears in clear on the cover and base. The U.S.

Glass Co. advertised similar ruby-flashed dishes in the 1890s and described them as suitable for cheese or butter.

Bennington Museum

18 | Sauce Dishes, Footed

Stemmed and footed sauce dishes are a late-Victorian form. Consequently, it is very rare to find any such piece in flint glass. The use of a lime-formula glass, however, need not be a sign of lesser quality. As with other pressed items, what is important is the degree of precision brought to the making of the mold and the act of pressing itself. By the late 1800s, the techniques developed in both phases of the operation had been considerably improved.

All of the examples illustrated here were made as parts of pattern sets. Among them are: Diamond Quilted, Westward Ho, Daisy and Button with Fan, Inverted Fan and Feather, and Paneled Hobnail. Of these, Westward Ho is the most famous. Introduced by Gillinder and Sons of Philadelphia shortly after the Centennial in the 1870s, it proved an almost instant success with the public. The pattern name was originally Pioneer, and the design is said to have been based on Currier and Ives Western scenes depicted in the famous prints. The frosted finish, also used for many other late patterns, is often explained as a means of hiding imperfections in the lime glass. More likely, it was used simply to enhance the representational relief patterns.

18-O Sauce Dishes (color plate, far left and far right)
Maker unknown, 1880s
Light blue, non-flint
2¼" H., 4¾" D.

Diamond Quilted pattern footed dishes with plain rims and circular bases; made in a variety of colors, including amber, canary, clear.

Sauce Dish (second from left)
Maker unknown, 1880s-90s
Amber, non-flint
3⅞" D.

Possibly Daisy and Button with Fan pattern; scalloped rim.

Sauce Dish (third from left)
Gillinder and Sons, Philadelphia, 1870s
Frosted, non-flint
3½" D.

Westward Ho pattern footed dish, with turned stem, plain rim, and frosted sides. Pattern also referred to as "Pioneer."

Bennington Museum

18-1 Sauce Dish
Indiana Glass Co., Indiana, Pa., 1890s
Emerald green with gilt accents, non-flint
2½" H.

Inverted Fan and Feather pattern sauce dish designed by Harry Northwood.

Bennington Museum

18-2 Sauce Dishes
Maker unknown, 1880s
Amber, non-flint
2¼" H., 4" D.

Paneled Hobnail pattern dishes with scalloped rims and plain bases.

Bennington Museum

18-3 Sauce Dish
Maker unknown, 1880s-90s
Light green, non-flint
2¼" H., 4" D.

Pattern not identified; stippled background in imitation of lacy glass.

Bennington Museum

19 | Butter Dishes

We have become so used to storing and serving butter in oblong dishes that it comes as a surprise to discover the round form common in the 19th century. The packaging of commercial butter in pound rectangles and quarter-pound sticks is a modern practice. Round, covered butter dishes became standard with the introduction of pattern-glass sets in the mid-1800s. Sometimes there were several varieties or forms within a pattern, as is illustrated in the Horn of Plenty examples (19-0 and 19-3). The differences may occur in the type of decoration or in the treatment of the base or the knob. The diameter of the various examples varies little—from six inches to approximately

7½ inches. The height is more variable, although six inches appears to be standard for many late pieces.

The Stippled Medallion butter dish (19-2) illustrates one of the most interesting phenomena in pressed glass manufacture—the continuing use of flint glass after the lime formula was introduced. Most objects in the Stippled Medallion pattern are found in lime glass, but the maker, possibly the Union Glass Co. of Somerville, Mass., obviously used both formulas during the period from 1860 to 1880.

The Peacock Feather pattern butter dish illustrated in color provides an example of yet another common practice in the trade—that of reworking old patterns near the end of the 19th century. This piece obviously is no kin to the heavy, flint, lacy piece of the 1830s and '40s. In this instance, however, there is no attempt to slavishly copy for the purpose of deceiving the buyer. Most imitation lacy dishes produced in the 1890s and early 1900s are simply variations on an old theme and should be judged on their own merits.

19-O Butter Dish (color plate, left to right)
Boston and Sandwich Glass Co., 1850s
Clear
Dish, 6⅛" D., cover, 5½" D.

Horn of Plenty pattern covered dish with acorn knob. See 19-2 for knob with head of Washington. A plain, flattened knob also exists.

Butter Dish
Maker unknown, 1880s-90s
Opalescent vaseline, non-flint
3½" H., 7⅝" D.

Unidentified basket weave type of pattern with a grape or maple leaf on cover.

Butter Dish
United States Glass Co, Pittsburgh, 1898-1900
Clear, non-flint
6½" H., 7" D.

Peacock Feather pattern from the turn-of-the-century which bears little resemblance to the lacy flint pattern of much earlier.

Bennington Museum

19-1 Butter Dish
Pittsburgh area, or Boston and Sandwich Glass Co., 1850s
Clear
6" H., 7" D.

Raised Petal and Loop pattern, one of the most graceful of mid-19th-

century glass designs; acorn knob.

Nancy Olsson Antiques
Durham, Pa.

19-2 Butter Dish

Maker unknown, 1860s
Clear
6" D.

Stippled Medallion pattern with heart-shaped knob. The pattern is most commonly found in non-flint glass.

Robertson and Thornton Antiques
Doylestown, Pa.

19-3 Butter Dish
M'Kee and Bros., or Boston and Sandwich Glass Co., 1850s
Clear
4⅛" H., 6" D.

Horn of Plenty pattern (Sandwich) or Comet pattern (M'Kee), an imitation of the original Sandwich design. Washington-head knob makes this piece especially rare.

Bennington Museum

19-4 Butter Dish
Midwestern, 1880s
Clear, non-flint
6" H., 7" D.

Shrine pattern with star and crescent panels alternating with teardrop

or petal. Probably made only in clear.

Ren's Antiques
Newtown, Pa.

20 | **Serving Plates and Platters**

Production of large-size serving dishes, as with butter dishes, began to a limited extent in the the mid-1800s. There are, of course, exceptional pieces, such as the open-handled lacy plate in a shell design (20-1), which date from an earlier time. The exact use or purpose of these lacy pieces, however, is unknown. They would appear to have been made principally for their decorative value.

The various bread plates (20-0, 20-2, 20-3) are in a class by themselves. The "Give Us This Day Our Daily Bread" theme was a natural one considering the religious climate of the time. There are many different treatments of this traditional message. The Willow Oak plate (20-0) and the Barley piece (20-3) are typical of pieces from late pattern-glass sets. All of these objects have size in common—running from nine to thirteen inches in length or diameter.

Portrait plates in large sizes—ten inches in the case of the U.S. Grant Peace Plate (20-5), and 11½ inches for the Grover Cleveland plate (20-0)—became popular in the 1880s. Some were obviously inspired by political campaigns and intended as souvenirs; others are commemorative. Whether they were even **used** on special occasions is a question that cannot be answered.

From evidence of remaining dishes, it seems clear that large-size glass serving plates and platters were only infrequently made. It is possible that the public was reluctant to use such a highly breakable material, and relied instead on china and silver plate. Even standard glass plates were rarely used in the home, except for dessert.

20-O Bread Plate (color plate, left)
Bryce Bros., Pittsburgh, 1870s
Clear, non-flint
9" D.

Willow Oak pattern with closed handles. Stippled background in oblong panels decorated with oak leaves; English daisy medallion in center. Also known in amber and blue.

Serving Plate (right)
Pittsburgh area, 1884
Frosted, non-flint
11½" D.

Grover Cleveland portrait plate made during the 1884 presidential campaign. The medallion is frosted. The border alternates with Button and Daisy pattern arches and semicircular arches with oak leaves. An identical plate was made for the vice-presidential candidate who ran with Cleveland, Thomas A. Hendricks. There are also identically designed James G. Blaine and John A. Logan plates which represent the Republican opposition in the 1884 campaign.

Bennington Museum

20-1 Open-Handled Dish
Boston and Sandwich Glass Co., c. 1820-30
Lacy, clear
9¼" W., including handle

Peacock Eye pattern shell dish with an open handle. A closed handle design in the Hairpin pattern was also produced in lacy glass by Sandwich. Both are great rarities.

Bennington Museum

20-2 Bread Plate
Maker unknown, late 1800s or early 1900s
Clear, non-flint
12" D.

Bread plate with unidentified pattern. Traditional "GIVE US THIS DAY OUR DAILY BREAD" message and wheat flowers in shoulder; sheaf of wheat in center.

Bennington Museum

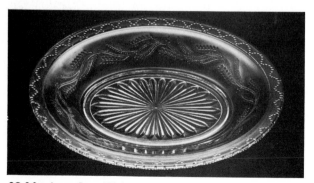

20-3 Serving or Bread Plate

Campbell, Jones & Co., 1880s
Clear, non-flint
9½" W., 11½" L.

Barley pattern with rayed center. This oval plate could have been intended for serving bread.

Bennington Museum

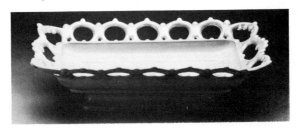

20-4 Serving Dish/Platter
Atterbury & Co., Pittsburgh, 1870s-80s
Turquoise blue milk glass, non-flint
3¼" H., 8" W., 13" L.

A plain serving dish with chain edge. Most of the Atterbury wares in opal ware or milk glass were opaque white, but they were also available in crystal, amber, blue, and mosaic.

Bennington Museum

20-5 U. S. Grant Peace Plate

Adams & Co., Pittsburgh, c. 1885
Light blue, non-flint
10" D.

Maple Leaf or Leaf pattern circular plate with serrated border; inscribed "LET US HAVE PEACE/U. S. GRANT". In the center surrounding the Grant portrait is inscribed: "Born April 27 1822/Died July 23 1885". Also available in apple green, yellow, amber, and clear.

Bennington Museum

21 | Standard Plates

Plates ranging in size from six inches to ten inches in diameter were produced from the 1830s through the end of the century. Those in the six-inch and seven-inch diameter category are generally known as tea plates and were among the first pattern wares made available in the 1850s. Typical of this variety are 21-1, 21-2, and 21-3. A later version, the Wheat and Barley pattern, 21-7, is also a tea plate. This type of dish was generally used for the serving of small cakes or other confections at teatime. The Roman Rosette pattern plate, 21-5, is of the same size but was not offered as part of a set.

The other plates, including most of the larger ones up to ten inches in diameter, are commemorative items or plates used on special occasions. The lacy examples are among the most handsome of pieces made by Sandwich. Two of these, the octagonal Beehive pattern and the Feather pattern, are illustrated in color.

21-O Plate (color plate, from left to right)
Indiana area, 1890s
Clear, non-flint
10" D.

Feather pattern plate with rayed center. This design is also known as Finecut and Feather and as Indiana Swirl. Lee states that it was originally named Doric. Available also in emerald green.

Plate
Boston and Sandwich Glass Co., 1830-60
Lacy, clear
1½" H., 9⅛" D. across flats, 9⅞" D. across points

Octagonal Beehive pattern dish or plate, commonly used by Sandwich as a bowl for a compote. One of the most popular designs, taking its name from center circle of beehives and bees. In the shoulder are found such motifs as acanthus leaves, grapes, thistles, and stars. Lee indicates that the dish was made as late as 1859. It appears only to have been made in clear. Reproductions abound, few of which will display any wear on the serrated rim.

Plate
Boston and Sandwich Glass Co., 1830-45
Lacy, clear
9" D.

Feather pattern variant plate with quatrefoil ornament in center. A Sawtooth border extends from the Feather pattern to a serrated rim.

Bennington Museum

21-1 Plate
Attributed to Boston and Sandwich Glass Co., Mid-1800s
Lacy, clear
6" D.

A tea-plate size in an unidentified pattern. Because the scalloped rim is relatively smooth and even, this may be a later lacy piece.

Nancy Olsson Antiques
Durham, Pa.

21-2 Plate
Boston and Sandwich Glass Co., c. 1850
Deep amethyst
6" D.

Bigler pattern tea plate in a standard six-inch size. Bigler was one of the

earliest distinct Sandwich patterns, but was also made by others. The color is extremely rare. Bigler, according to Lee, is found most often in goblets and cordials.

Bennington Museum

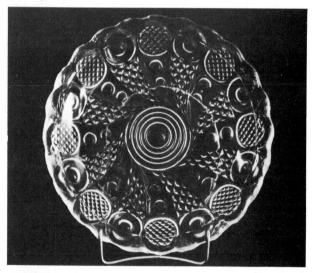

21-3 Plate
Boston and Sandwich Glass Co., 1850s
Clear

¾" H., 6⁵⁄₁₆" D.

Horn of Plenty pattern plate somewhat larger than tea size; center made up of concentric circles. Rim is scalloped in a plain style.

Bennington Museum

21-4 Plate
Boston and Sandwich Glass Co., c. 1837
Lacy, clear
6⅜" D.

Victoria coronation plate celebrating the crowning of the queen. The symbols of England, Scotland, and Ireland—the rose, thistle, and shamrock—are found in the border along with a crown. Tea-plate size.

Bennington Museum

21-5 Plate
Boston and Sandwich Glass Co., 1830-45
Clear
⅞" H., 6⅛" D.

Roman Rosette (early) pattern plate with chain-band border. Accord-

ing to McKearin, found also in deep amethyst and opalescent.

Bennington Museum

21-6 Plate
Boston and Sandwich Glass Co., c. 1832
Lacy, clear
5¾" D.

The George Washington pattern plate thought to have been issued by
Sandwich in commemoration of the 100th anniversary of Washington's
birth. Medallion is inscribed "WASHINGTON GEORGE" and is surrounded by wreath of acorns and leaves.

Bennington Museum

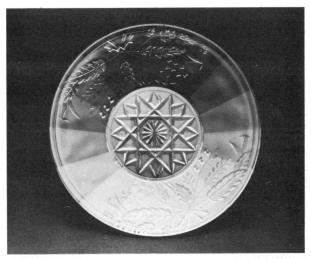

21-7 Plate
Bryce Bros., Pittsburgh, 1880s
Light blue, non-flint
7" D.

Wheat and Barley pattern, originally termed "Duquesne" by the manufacturer. Reissued by U. S. Glass Co. in 1898. Also found in amber, clear, and yellow.

Bennington Museum

22 | Trays

The collector looking for pressed glass trays is likely to find that these special items date from the last quarter of the 19th century. Consequently, almost all are of a non-flint variety and display one of the traditional pattern-glass designs such as Minerva (22-0), a diamond variant (22-1), Hobnail (22-2), and Frosted Lion (22-4). Some of the trays were made as part of a water set and came with two goblets, a pitcher, and perhaps a waste bowl. The Hobnail tray is of this variety. The commemorative bread tray (22-3) made by Gillinder and Sons, is included in this grouping (rather than in chapter 20) because of its unusually large size. It could easily hold a foot-long loaf. The probability, however, is that this piece was merely displayed on a shelf and never taken down for use, except on special occasions.

22-0 Tray (color plate)
Boston and Sandwich Glass Co., 1870s
Clear, non-flint
11" L.

Octagonal, closed-handle tray or platter in the Minerva pattern, so-named for the goddess of wisdom pictured in the center medallion.

Robertson and Thornton Antiques
Doylestown, Pa.

22-1 Tray
Maker unknown, Early 1900s
Clear, non-flint
14" L.

Diamond and fan design in shoulder of tray or dish; ray motif in center. Made in imitation of cut glass popular at the time.

Ren's Antiques
Newtown, Pa.

22-2 Tray
Attributed to Adams & Co., Pittsburgh, 1880s
Blue, non-flint
1" H., 11 5/8" D.

Hobnail pattern tray from a water set probably consisting of two tumblers and a pitcher. Sides are paneled.

Bennington Museum

22-3 Tray
Gillinder & Sons, Philadelphia, 1876
Clear, non-flint
13¼" L. from handle to handle

One of many bread trays designed and introduced during the Centennial year and exhibited in Philadelphia. This features the Bunker Hill Monument and reads (at top), "PRESCOTT 1776 STARK/THE HEROES OF BUNKER HILL/BIRTHPLACE OF LIBERTY" and (below), "WARREN 1876 THE SPIRIT OF SEVENTY SIX".

Bennington Museum

22-4 Tray
Gillinder & Sons, Philadelphia, 1860s

Clear
9½" L., 5½" W.

Frosted Lion pattern, so-named for unusual handles in frosted glass.

Robertson and Thornton Antiques
Doylestown, Pa.

23 | Cake Stands

A surprising number of 19th-century pressed glass cake stands and plates can be found today. This availability would seem to indicate that production was fairly widespread, at least during the period from 1870 to the early 20th century. Plain cake stands with a candlestick or pillar standard, such as 23-3, were made for bakeries as well as home use. In some late pattern sets, three different sizes of stands were offered—eight-inch, nine-inch, and ten-inch diameters. The Wildflower cake stand, 23-2, is typical of those made as part of pattern-glass sets.

Cake plates were available as early as the 1830s in a lacy design, and were offered intermittently for many years in simpler designs. Many of these plates have "cut" or folded corners which give the piece an unequal octagonal form.

23-O Cake Stand (color plate)
Maker unknown, Early 1900s
Clear, non-flint
4¼" H., 9" D.

Unidentified pattern of diamonds and petals; octagonal foot and ringed stem.

Ren's Antiques
Newtown, Pa.

23-1 Cake Plate
Boston and Sandwich Glass Co., 1830s-40s
Lacy, clear
9½" D.

Beehive pattern base with bees surrounding a hive; this motif is encircled by an alternating design of five-pointed stars and thistles. The shoulder design features shields, scrolls, and acanthus leaves and ter-

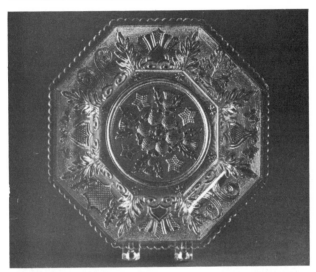

minates in a scalloped rim.

Bennington Museum

23-2 Cake Stand
Adams & Co., Pittsburgh, c. 1874
Canary, non-flint
6" H., 9½" D.

Wildflower pattern stand; inverted bowl base. Available also in clear crystal, amber, blue, apple green, and, reportedly, amethyst. Reissued in 1898 by United States Glass Co. as their "No. 140" pattern.

Bennington Museum

23-3 Cake Stand
Maker unknown, Mid-1800s
Clear
7" H., 9¼" D.

Plain cake stand with candlestick base.

Ren's Antiques
Newtown, Pa.

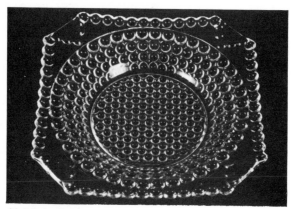

23-4 Cake Plate

Richards & Hartley, Tarentum, PA, 1870s-80s
Clear, non-flint
10" D.

Thousand-Eye pattern cake plate with folded corners. Plates were also produced in six- and eight-inch diameters. Colors are yellow, blue, opalescent, apple green, amber, light amber, and opaque blue.

Ren's Antiques
Newtown, Pa.

24 | Compotes and Sweetmeats

Compotes are among the most interesting and varied of Victorian pressed glass objects. There are hundreds of designs and sizes to choose from. Nearly every major and minor manufacturer produced them, and today a collector would have to be blind to miss them. Sweetmeat dishes are generally smaller in height and diameter and were usually covered, many of these covers having disappeared over time. A sweetmeat was intended to hold candy or candied fruit. The form appears to have been most popular during the mid-19th century, and was later replaced in popularity with a low-footed candy or bonbon dish. Consequently, sweetmeat dishes are considerably more difficult to find than compotes. A small flint glass sweetmeat which is round in shape, however, is often mistaken for a compote.

A compote, also sometimes termed a "comport" in the past by manufacturers affecting English ways, is simply a bowl with a standard or stem, and a foot or base. The bowl itself may be no different than the type offered without the additional parts to elevate it. The standard may closely resemble those used for candlesticks and lamps. The base or foot is usually quite simple and often is round or hexagonal in form.

The most colorful compotes date from the 1840-to-1860 period. Such striking colors as amethyst (as in 24-0) and canary with an opalescent hue (24-7) were featured. Most compotes, however, were probably produced in clear glass in both the flint- and lime-glass periods. The colors found in late-Victorian objects are lighter in shade—light yellow, blue, apple green.

Compotes appear to range from as small as 4½ inches, to ten inches high. Objects larger than this are probably more properly termed punch bowls; if they are smaller or lower, they may be sweetmeat dishes. The top diameter of the usual compote is larger than the height, and the shape may vary from round to oval. A compote made by Sandwich from 1850-70 in the Horn of Plenty pattern, 24-13, is nothing more than a raised, oval relish dish. Many compotes made later in the century are termed low-footed and have a short standard. Other compotes have no standard or stem at all, the bowl resting directly on a circular or hexagonal base; these strongly resemble berry or punch bowls. Another special late-Victorian form is that of the mounted compote, a bowl resting in a silver-plated stand (24-14).

24-O Pair of Compotes (color plate, left to right)
Boston and Sandwich Glass Co., 1840-50
Deep amethyst
8" H., 8⅜" top D.

Openwork compotes with hexagonal feet and knop stems. Color is very rare.

Compote
Boston and Sandwich Glass Co., c. 1840
Deep amethyst
5⅜" H., 7½" top D.

Petal and Loop pattern compote bowl with Petal and Loop pattern stem; circular foot. Color is very rare.

Bennington Museum

24-1 Covered Sweetmeat
Attributed to Pittsburgh area, 1850s
Clear
6¾" H. to to of finial

Thumbprint pattern cover, bowl, stem, and foot. Circular foot is scalloped; stem is octagonal.

Robertson and Thornton Antiques
Doylestown, Pa.

24-2 Compote
Maker unknown, 1850s
Clear
5" H., 6¼" top D.

Sawtooth pattern bowl with hexagonal stem and foot.

Frenchtown House of Antiques
Frenchtown, N.J.

24-3 Compote
Boston and Sandwich Glass Co., 1840-50
Clear

6¼" H., 9¼" top D.

Openwork compote on hexagonal foot and stem.

Bennington Museum

24-4 Sweetmeat
Bakewell, Pears & Co., Pittsburgh
1850s-60s
Clear
4⅝" H., 4⅞" top D.

Victoria pattern sweetmeat without cover; octagonal stem on plain circular foot.

Author's Collection

24-5 Compote
Attributed to New England Glass Co., Cambridge, Mass., 1850s
Clear
7¾" H., 8" top D.

Sawtooth pattern bowl with heavy, rough points; hexagonal stem on plain circular foot.

Author's Collection

24-6 Compote
M'Kee and Bros., Pittsburgh, 1860s
Clear
5½" H., 7¼" top D.

Prism pattern bowl with stem in same pattern, resting on plain circular foot.

Frenchtown House of Antiques
Frenchtown, N.J.

24-7 Compote
M'Kee and Bros., Pittsburgh, c. 1860
Canary with opalescent rim
4½" H., 6¼" at widest point

Petticoat Dolphin form dish popularized by M'Kee; resting on a plain

foot with concentric circles.

Bennington Museum

24-8 Compote

Boston and Sandwich Glass Co., 1860s
Clear
8" top D.

New England Pineapple pattern bowl and inverted bowl base. Compotes were produced in four sizes in this pattern.

Nancy Olsson Antiques
Durham, Pa.

24-9 Compote
Bryce Bros., Pittsburgh, 1860s
Clear
10¼" H., 11" top D.

Tulip pattern bowl with diamond band; hexagonal stem resting on plain circular foot.

Bennington Museum

24-10 Sweetmeat
Possibly Bakewell, Pears and Co., Pittsburgh, 1860s

Clear
4½" H., 6" top D.

Thumbprint pattern bowl and hexagonal stem tapering to plain circular foot; cover missing. Pattern was named "Argus" and sold by Bakewell, Pears.

Bennington Museum

24-11 Compote
Attributed to M'Kee and Bros., Pittsburgh, 1860s
Clear

4¾" H., 8¾" top D.

Bellflower pattern bowl resting directly on plain circular foot; scalloped rim. Also known, but rare, in sapphire blue, milk white, opalescent, and amber.

Bennington Museum

24-12 Compote
Pittsburgh area, c. 1875
Light amethyst
9¼" H., 11½" at widest point

Dolphin form compote with cut-out corners; leaf design around bowl; circular base.

Bennington Museum

24-13 Compote
Boston and Sandwich Glass Co., 1850s
Clear
6" H., 10" W.

Oval relish dish with added pedestal and foot, both in Horn of Plenty pattern. (See 15-2.)

Bennington Museum

24-14 Mounted Compote
Attributed to George Duncan & Sons, Pittsburgh, 1860s-70s
Amber, non-flint
5⅛" H., 9" D.

Tree of Life pattern, set in silver-plated stand. Since this pattern is ribbed, unlike that illustrated in 24-16, the attribution to Pittsburgh seems a safe one.

Bennington Museum

24-15 Compote
Portland Glass Co., Portland, Me.; or George Duncan & Sons, Pittsburgh, 1870s-80s
Clear, non-flint
6⅜" H., 6⅞" D.

Tree of Life or Shell and Tassel pattern with the name "Davis" etched in the design. William O. Davis was the superintendent of the Portland plant in the late 1860s and early '70s, but went to work for Duncan after the closing of the Maine company in 1873. Duncan manfactured both a round and a square form, as illustrated here.

Bennington Museum

24-16 Compote
Portland Glass Co., Portland,
   Me., 1860s-70s
Clear, non-flint
6⅜" H., 6⅞" D.

This compote or epergne is clearly
a product of the Portland Glass
Co. A figure of a child forms the
standard; the stepped base is octagonal.

Bennington Museum

24-17 Compote
Campbell, Jones & Co., Pittsburgh, 1880s
Canary, non-flint
5" H., 7¾" at widest point

Rose Sprig pattern bowl and hexagonal foot; irregular rim. Also
available in clear, blue, and amber.

Bennington Museum

24-18 Compote
Maker unknown, Early 1900s
Milk glass
7¾" H., 6¾" top D.

Scalloped bowl in Grape pattern, on ribbed circular stem and foot.

Frenchtown House of Antiques
Frenchtown, N.J.

24-19 Compote
Maker unknown, 1880s
Light blue, non-flint
7¾" D.

Raindrop pattern bowl on circular base. Also available in amber,

yellow, clear, and apple green.
Bennington Museum

25 | Celery Vases

Vases intended for holding celery stalks are an anomaly today, the relish dish having long ago replaced the vase in general use. Almost any celery vase, however, is more attractive in decoration and form than the lowly dish. Especially handsome are those made from 1840-70 by both New England and Pittsburgh-area glass factories. The vase was often termed a holder and was a standard part of a typical pattern-glass set. The height of the average piece, nine to ten inches, closely approximates that of a vase meant to hold flowers, but the stem on the celery is shorter and often resembles that found on a goblet. The bowls of the celery vases are usually somewhat fuller and less tapered.

The first celery vases in pressed glass are in patterns such as Four-Printie-Block (25-0) and Circle and Gothic Arch (25-0), which were popular before the advent of tableware sets. These same patterns were available in such other forms as candlesticks, flower vases, lamps, and footed tumblers. The range of colors—canary, amethyst, blue purple, emerald green—is somewhat less extensive in celery vases. The pattern-set vases which follow them in age, such as the

Thumbprint (25-1), Sawtooth (25-2), and Horn of Plenty (25-3), are generally available only in clear glass.

The production of celery vases continued into the non-flint period of the 1870s and '80s, the Jacob's Ladder piece being typical (25-4). Gradually, however, the vase lost its stem and foot, as in the Manhattan pattern object made by the U.S. Glass Co. (25-5).

25-O Celery Vase (color plate, left)
Boston and Sandwich Glass Co., c. 1840
Canary 10¼" H., 5" D.

Four-Printie-Block pattern, scalloped top, hexagonal base, and knob stem.

Celery Vase (right)
Boston and Sandwich Glass Co., 1840-50
Clear
10" H., 5½" D.

Circle and Gothic Arch pattern vase resting on hexagonal stem and round foot. The rim is heavily scalloped.

Bennington Museum

25-1 Celery Vase
Bakewell, Pears and Co.
Pittsburgh, 1860s
Clear
9½" H., 5⅜" D.

Thumbprint pattern vase, one of two styles produced in this design originally named "Argus" by Bakewell, Pears. The knob stem is a distinct characteristic of the firm's work.

Bennington Museum

25-2 Pair of Celery Vases
New England area, 1860s
Clear
9" H., 4½" D.

Sawtooth pattern vases with hexagonal and knob stems. Each round
foot is rayed, as was common with early ware in this pattern.

Author's Collection

25-3 Celery Vase
Boston and Sandwich Glass Co.
1850s
Clear
8¾" H.

Horn of Plenty vase with scalloped rim and hexagonal knob stem; foot is round.

Bennington Museum

25-4 Celery Vase
Bryce Bros., Pittsburgh, 1870s
Clear, non-flint
9" H.

Jacob's Ladder pattern vase with knob stem and rayed foot. The pattern was known as "Maltese" by its maker.

Frenchtown House of Antiques
Frenchtown, N.J.

25-5 Celery Vase
United States Glass Co.
   Pittsburgh, c. 1904
Clear, non-flint
6" H.

Manahattan pattern vase with wide and scalloped rim. Illustrated in the firm's 1904 catalogue. The pattern is thought to date from two years earlier.

Ren's Antiques
Newtown, Pa.

26 | Pitchers

A water pitcher was an important item in a pattern-glass set. Sometimes three different sizes were offered: pint, quart, and half-gallon. The last size, however, seems to have been the most commonly produced. Pitchers of this sort could also be purchased as part of a water set consisting of two glasses, a waste bowl, and a tray.

The early glass companies had much experience in making blown three-mold pitchers and continued to produce such wares along with pressed items. Not until the post-Civil War period did any manufacturer attempt a completely pressed pitcher, that is, one in which the handle, as well as the main body of the piece, were pressed. The usual handle used before this time was a blown piece which was applied, the Sawtooth pattern pitcher (26-0) and the Cable pattern pitcher (26-1) being representative of this method.

Flint glass pitchers of the pre-1870 period are especially brilliant, appealing pieces, but striking effects were also possible in lime glass. The Baltimore Pear pattern (26-2) is one of the favorite designs of the late Victorian period. The various products of the Heisey company are also highly collectible today, the crystal being of a hard and particularly pure quality. Lemonade pitchers are a special variety made in the '90s and at the turn of the century. Like many later water pitchers, they are low-footed, or have no base at all.

26-O Water Pitcher
New England area, 1860-70
Clear
9" H., 5½" D.

Sawtooth pattern pitcher in the half-gallon size; footed and with applied handle.

Water Pitcher
Gillinder and Bennett, Pittsburgh, 1860s
Clear
9¼" H. to top of handle

Honeycomb pattern pitcher in a half-gallon size; footed and with pressed handle.

Water Pitcher
New England area, 1860s
Clear
8½" H.

New England Pineapple pattern pitcher; footed and with applied handle.

Bennington Museum

26-1 Water Pitcher

Boston and Sandwich Glass Co., 1850s
Clear
9½" H.

Cable pattern pitcher with applied handle; made to commemorate the laying of the transatlantic cable.

Bennington Museum

26-2 Water Pitcher
Adams & Co., Pittsburgh, c. 1875
Clear, non-flint
8" H.

Baltimore Pear pattern, known as Gipsy by its manufacturer; octagonal foot and blown, applied handle. Widely reproduced in the 20th century, some with the pear stained.

Ren's Antiques
Newtown, Pa.

26-3 Water Pitcher
United States Glass Co.
** Pittsburgh, 1890s**
Clear, non-flint
8" H.

Jewel with Dewdrop pattern; named "Kansas" by its maker. Foot and rim are scrolled. There are six stippled and six clear panels.

Bennington Museum

26-4 Lemonade Pitcher and Tumblers
South Jersey area, c. 1900-1910
Clear, decorated with cranberry enamel; non-flint
Pitcher, 10" H.; tumblers, each 4" H.

Unidentified pattern. The decoration has been applied by hand.

Robertson and Thornton Antiques
Doylestown, Pa.

26-5 Water Pitcher
A. H. Heisey & Co., Neward, Ohio, Early 1900s
Clear
6½" H. to top of handle

Unidentified pattern signed "Heisey."

Ren's Antiques
Newtown, Pa.

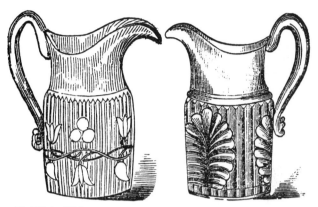

26-6 Water Pitchers
M'Kee and Brothers, Pittsburgh, 1871
Clear
Half-gallon size

Left, Ribbed Leaf or Bellflower pattern; right, Sprig or Ribbed Palm pattern. These were two of the most popular M'Kee patterns from the 1860s and early '70s. Handles are applied in both examples. M'Kee preferred the names Ribbed Leaf and Sprig. M'Kee also produced syrup pitchers in these patterns, which from all appearances seem to be molded rather than pressed. Usually found only in clear. Illustrated in the 1871 M'Kee catalogue.

26-7 Water Pitcher
M'Kee and Brothers, Pittsburgh
1868
Clear
Quart size

26-8 Water Pitcher
M'Kee and Brothers, Pittsburgh
1864
Clear
Half-gallon size

Prism pattern quart water pitcher. A second half-gallon size was also illustrated in the 1868 catalogue.

Stedman or Blaze pattern half-gallon water pitcher; Stedman was the name used by M'Kee. The

Bakewell, Pears & Co. of Pittsburgh also produced a Prism pattern dating from the 1870s and made in non-flint. It features a fluted band and often includes engraving.

New England Glass Co., Cambridge, Mass., illustrated the same pattern, Blaze, in their 1869 catalogue. Lee, however, points out that the ribbing on the New England pieces is much finer and that all the M'Kee forms with stems have rayed rather than plain bases. For the most part, this appears to be true. The object illustrated here is from the 1864 M'Kee Catalogue.

27 | Syrups

Syrup jugs or pitchers appear to have been more widely made and used after the Civil War than before. They were produced in flint glass by at least one Pittsburgh-area company, M'Kee and Brothers, in the Stedman and the Bellflower patterns, but these are exceptions. Syrups do not appear in the published list of forms for almost any other early pattern. Most probably, small pint pitchers without lids served the same purpose.

The syrup containers illustrated here all have metal, hinged tops—sometimes of pewter, other times of tinned iron. A special pouring lid, visible in 27-0, was also important for the viscous liquid. Molasses was the most frequently used syrup, and the jugs often went by that name in late-Victorian glass catalogues.

27-O Syrup Pitcher (color plate)
Attributed to New England Glass Co., Cambridge, Mass., 1860s
Clear
7¼" H. with top

Knives and Forks pattern pitcher with pewter top and pouring lid. The handle is blown-molded.

Robertson and Thornton Antiques
Doylestown, Pa.

27-1 Syrup Pitcher
Pittsburgh area, 1870s-80s
Blue with opalescent, non-flint
6½" H., 3⅞" D.

Inverted Thumbprint pattern, pear-shaped syrup pitcher with

27-2 Syrup Pitcher
Maker unknown, 1880s-90s
Clear, with amber-stained panels, non-flint
6¼" H., 3¾" D.

Covered pitcher in unidentified

ovals in opalescent. Handle is clear blue and applied and the top is tinned iron with collar and spout of the same material. The cover is spring-loaded.

Bennington Museum

pattern with three clear panels featuring a sunburst design. Cover is nickel-plated and hinged.

Bennington Museum

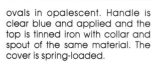

27-3 Syrup Pitcher
Pittsburgh area, c. 1900
Clear, non-flint
7½" H., 3" D.

Covered pitcher in Forty-four pattern with metal cover and tip.

Bennington Museum

28 | Cream Pitchers

Cream pitchers, along with sugar bowls, are basic forms produced in pressed glass from the 1830s on. At least in lacy glass, however, it is unlikely that a collector can find matching pieces. The variety of patterns in early glass is also fairly limited. By the 1850s, when sets of tableware were being produced, the number of patterns increased dramatically.

The lacy-period pieces, illustrations 28-0 through 28-1, are very rich in symbols—the acanthus leaf, shield, hearts, Gothic arches, guilloche—and fine stippling. Most of the objects appear to have been made by the Sandwich firm, an association which is suggested by the delicate detailing; even the handles are stippled in some examples. The opaque pitchers, 28-0, far right, and 28-1, were probably made at a later time than the clear pieces.

Representative of early pattern-glass pitchers, available in sets of tableware or separately, are the Horn of Plenty (28-3) and Four-Petal (28-2) creamers. Creamers were made, sometimes in two different sizes, in all the mid-century patterns. All are footed and many have crimped handles.

Creamers of a later date are made of a non-flint glass in a low-footed style or, as in the case of the Printed Hobnail pattern example (28-4), without a foot or base. Handles are usually pressed along with the body of the piece.

28-O Cream Pitcher (color plate, left to right)
Maker unknown, 1830s-40s
Lacy clear
4¼" H.

Alice Hulett Metz calls this pattern early Heart; no other documentation has been found. Stippled hearts are placed to each side of the lip, and stars surround the rim. The design is that of a half-moon or drape. The base is round and plain.

Cream Pitcher
Boston and Sandwich Glass Co., 1830-45
Lacy, clear
4¼" H.

Acanthus Leaf and Shield pattern creamer with octagonal scalloped foot and stippled handle.

Cream Pitcher
Boston and Sandwich Glass Co., 1830-45
Lacy, clear
4" H.

Peacock Feather pattern is found above and the Gothic Arch and Palm pattern below. Scalloped foot and stippled handle.

Cream Pitcher
Boston and Sandwich Glass Co., 1830-45
Opaque blue
4¼" H.

Guilloche design above and a Gothic Arch and Palm pattern below; scalloped rim and foot.

Bennington Museum

28-1 Cream Pitcher
Maker unknown, 1850s-60s
Opaque white
4½" H.

Identical to object illustrated in 28-0.

Robertson and Thornton Antiques Doylestown, Pa.

28-2 Cream Pitcher
Maker unknown, 1850s
Clear
6¼" H.

Four-Petal pattern creamer with fluted top, round foot, and applied handle.

Bennington Museum

28-3 Cream Pitcher
Boston and Sandwich Glass Co., 1860s
Clear
6½" H., 3⅜" D.

Horn of Plenty pattern creamer; larger of two sizes made by Sandwich. Scalloped foot and crimped handle.

Bennington Museum

28-4 Cream Pitcher
Maker unknown, 1880s
Clear
5" H.

Printed Hobnail pattern creamer with plain top and spout. Printed Hobnail was also made in amethyst, blue, yellow, and amber. The pattern is sometimes called "Strawberry."

Frenchtown House of Antiques
Frenchtown, N.J.

28-5 Cream Pitcher
**Challinor, Taylor & Co., or
    U.S. Glass Co., Pittsburgh**
1880s-90s
Milk glass, non-flint
3½" H.

Ear of Corn pattern pitcher, the smaller of two sizes first produced by Challinor, Taylor in 1888 and reissued by U.S. Glass after 1891.

Bennington Museum

28-6 Cream Pitcher
Bryce Bros., Pittsburgh, 1870s
Clear, non-flint
6¼" H.

Jacob's Ladder or Maltese pattern creamer with knob stem and round foot.

Frenchtown House of Antiques
Frenchtown, N.J.

29 | Sugar Bowls

Many admirers of pressed glass find this form the most interesting of all to collect. But to find a sugar bowl with the right cover—intact—requires considerable perseverance. Sugar bowls, like creamers, were standard pieces in the 19th-century glassmaker's repertoire. Despite this familiarity, these practical objects were often imbued with exceptional artistry. The famous Ihmsen sugar bowl (29-3) is one such unusual piece.

The nine sides and cover of the Ihmsen salesman's sample sugar bowl contain illustrations of the firm's products in the early 1850s. Shown on the piece are a tumbler, ale glass, spill holder, candlestick, square bowl, decanter, champagne, inkwell, salt, goblet, and compote; the Ashburton, Flute, and Excelsior patterns are exhibited in various combinations around the piece. The molds used for pressing the cover and the bowl were clearly cast with great care to assure the visibility of these details.

The other early- and mid-19th century sugar bowls are not quite as ambitious in design, but almost any one of them could have served as an effective sample. The colorful lacy and partially stippled bowls of the 1830s and '40s remain the favorites of glass collectors. They feature the geometric patterns popular during the period. The Four-Petal (29-5), Sweetheart (29-6), Cable with Ring (29-7), New England Pineapple (29-8), and Lee (29-10) covered bowls are similar in form to the lacy-period pieces, but the striking colors are absent.

The many-sided traditional form gradually faded away in the late 19th century to be replaced with simple round bowls or even cups (such as 29-11), distinguished only by such decorative touches as frosting or staining. There was, however, a revival of interest in so-called "Colonial" patterns in the early 1900s. These footed imitations are not without interest today, but they lack the imaginative design and the brilliance of finish exhibited in the past.

29-0 Sugar Bowls (color plate, left to right)
Boston and Sandwich Glass Co., 1830s-40s
Turquoise, clambroth, and canary
Each is 5½" H. with cover, 4⅝" D.

Gothic Arch pattern sugar bowls of the New England variety. Each is partially stippled, octagonal-shaped, and has a solid foot.

Bennington Museum

29-1 Sugar Bowl
Boston and Sandwich Glass Co.
1830-45
Lacy, clear
5¾" H. to top of finial, 4¾" D.

Acanthus Leaf and Shield pattern base and Palm pattern cover. Scalloped foot, rim of cover, and knob or finial.

Bennington Museum

29-2 Sugar Bowl
Pittsburgh area, 1830s-40s
Lacy, clear
5½" H., 4⅝" D.

Gothic Arch pattern sugar bowl of the type made in the Pittsburgh area. It differs from the Sandwich variety in having less stippling and a less overall lacy design. Different designs may be used in the eight panels of the cover and base.

Robertson and Thornton Antiques
Doylestown, Pa.

29-3 Sugar Bowl
C. Ihmsen, Pittsburgh, 1851
Clear
3½" H. without cover, 4¾" D.

A sugar bowl in the distinctive Ihmsen pattern with nine Gothic arch panels showing different samples of the company's work. This was made as a salesman's sample.

Bennington Museum

29-4 Sugar Bowl
Boston and Sandwich Glass Co.
1850s
Deep amethyst
10" H. to top of finial

Petal and Loop pattern hexagonal sugar bowl with acorn finial top.

Bennington Museum

29-5 Sugar Bowl
Maker unknown, 1850s
Clear
7½" H. to finial; base, 4" D.

Four-Petal pattern covered sugar bowl, one of two known forms, the other without the foot.

Bennington Museum

29-6 Sugar Bowl
Boston and Sandwich Glass Co., 1840s-50s
Clear
9" H. to top of finial, 5" D.

Sweetheart pattern, hexagonal covered sugar bowl; hexagonal stem and round foot.

Nancy Olsson Antiques
Durham, Pa.

29-7 Sugar Bowl
Boston and Sandwich Glass Co., 1850s
Clear
7¼" H. to top of finial

Cable with Ring pattern covered sugar bowl. The pattern is sometimes termed Cable with Ring and Star, a star being found on the bottom of the base. Even the base is encircled with a cable design. Lee calls it an "elaboration" on the standard Cable pattern.

Bennington Museum

29-8 Sugar Bowl
Attributed to New England Glass Co., Cambridge, Mass., 1860s
Clear
8¾" H. to top of finial

Covered sugar bowl in New England Pineapple pattern, one of two known styles; hexagonal stem and clear, round base.

Bennington Museum

29-9 Sugar Bowl
C. Ihmsen & Co., Pittsburgh
1850s
Light canary
4½″ H. with top; 4¼″ D.

Small, covered sugar bowl in Ihmsen pattern; octagonal form without stem; scalloped rim on bowl.

Nancy Olsson Antiques
Durham, Pa.

29-11 Sugar Bowl
Doyle and Co., Pittsburgh, 1880s
Clear, ruby-stained, non-flint
4¼" H.

Triple Triangle pattern in ruby-stained ware manufactured in Pittsburgh area and Midwestern glass factories from the 1880s to early 1900s. This example might be better termed a twin-handled cup or mug. Reissued by U.S. Glass after 1891 as "No. 76" pattern.

Bennington Museum

29-10 Sugar Bowl
Pittsburgh area, or Sandwich
1850s-60s
Clear
8¼" H. to top of finial

Lee pattern, named for Ruth Webb Lee. The design features elongated petal panels, scalloped octagonal stem, and clear, round base.

Robertson and Thornton Antiques
Doylestown, Pa.

30 | **Finger Bowls**

Bowls clearly identified as being finger bowls are rarely encountered today. Their production was limited in comparison to such standard items as berry and serving bowls of various sizes. It is possible that bowls of a smaller diameter, five inches or less, could be used either as finger bowls or individual serving dishes. The use of the finger bowl at the table appears to have been more prevalent toward the end of the century than earlier. Nearly all the patterns illustrated in the 1904 United States Glass Co. catalogue for example, include this item.

The cased or overlay pair of finger bowls (30-0) may have been a special order item. As noted in the entry, the technique of overlaying color on clear glass was used primarily for lamps (see 2-4) at Sandwich.

30-0 Pair of Fingerbowls (color plate)
Boston and Sandwich Glass Co., 1850s-60s
Cased or overlaid with gold ruby on clear
2⅞" H., 5¼" D. at top

No known pattern name. It was unusual for finger bowls to be decorated in this manner, a technique most often used for lamp fonts, perfume bottles, and paperweights.

Bennington Museum

30-1 Finger Bowl
United States Glass Co.,
  Pittsburgh, 1904-1910
Crystal
Dimensions unknown

Columbia pattern, reissued by U.S. Glass Co. after 1891 and included in the 1904 catalogue. The pattern originated with the Colombia Glass Co., Findlay, Ohio, c. 1888, a company absorbed by U.S. Glass and known as "Factory J." From the U.S. Glass Co., 1904 catalogue.

30-2 Finger Bowl
United States Glass Co.,
  Pittsburgh, 1904-1910
Crystal
Dimensions unknown

Michigan pattern, one of U.S. Glass Co.'s six "battleship" patterns, this first issued c. 1893. Gilt trim. From the U.S. Glass Co., 1904 catalogue.

31 | Punch Bowls

Punch bowls with a plain rim foot have been made in silver and in pottery and porcelain since the 17th century. Only in the 19th century did it become common to find them of glass. At first the form was almost indistinguishable from that of a compote, the bowl not resting directly on the rim, but raised on a standard. The Bakewell, Pears punch bowls (31-1 and 31-2) are designated for this purpose because of their large diameter. Later bowls more closely approximate the traditional form, as does 31-0. One of the most attractive punch-bowl sets dates from the 1880s and '90s in the Inverted Thumprint pattern. This pattern is also known as Polka Dot, or Dot. A number of Pittsburgh and Wheeling companies were responsible for the bulk of production. The colors—cranberry, yellow, blue, amber, green—are especially pleasing.

31-O Punch Bowl (color plate)
Maker unknown, Early 1900s
Clear, non-flint
10" H. with stand, 14¼" D.

An unidentified pattern featuring a chrysanthemum and thistle design. The bowl rests on a stand.

Ren's Antiques
Newtown, Pa.

31-1 Punch Bowl
Bakewell, Pears & Co., Pittsburgh, 1860s
Clear
12" H. , 14" D.

Thumbprint pattern identical in every respect to 31-2. Diameter of bowl is greater, but the object was clearly intended to be used for the same purpose.

Bennington Museum

31-2 Covered Compote or Punch Bowl
Bakewell, Pears & Co., Pittsburgh, 1860s
Clear
15½" H. with cover, 8" D.

Thumbprint pattern covered compote which is large enough to have
been used as a punch bowl. Thumbprint went by the trade name of
"Argus."

Bennington Museum

32 | Bowls

The bowl form was central to the production of 19th-century pressed glass. It is rare, nonetheless, to find an object listed simply as a "bowl" in the various compilations of pattern sets. A bowl might be a compote (high or low-footed), a berry dish, a nappy, a sauce dish, or even a finger bowl. The type being described in this chapter is basically a serving bowl of a large size—from eight to ten inches in diameter. Only the openwork example, 32-0, is smaller. It is included here because it is an early piece made at a time when bowls, as such, were usually not designated for some special purpose. An openwork piece might hold fruit or be used for other decorative foods.

Lacy bowls from the 1830-45 period, such as 32-1, were made in small and large sizes. They are essentially deep dishes, and because of their beauty, it is hard to conceive of them being used for more than special occasions. Nearly all the customary lacy designs—Princess Feather, Tulip and Acanthus Leaf, Dahlia, Oak Leaf, and Gothic Arch —are to be found. Like the plates—standard size and cup-plate size— of the period, the rims are usually serrated, scalloped, or beaded in some manner.

Pattern-glass serving bowls vary from the very early Inverted Heart (32-2), shown with the model used in making the mold, to the late Daisy example (32-2), whose design is intended to imitate cut glass.

32-0 Bowl (color plate, left to right)
Maker unknown, c. 1840
Red
5½" D.

Openwork bowl, perhaps a product of the Boston and Sandwich Glass Co.

Bowl
Boston and Sandwich Glass Co., c. 1850
Canary
3⅜" H., 10" D.

Oval Mitre pattern bowl, made for use (with a stem and foot added) as a compote; scalloped rim.

Bowl
Boston and Sandwich Glass Co., c. 1840
Sapphire blue
8" D.

Seven-sided bowl in Petal and Loop pattern; sapphire shading toward clear in petals. Available also in other colors.

Bennington Museum

32-1 Serving Bowl
Boston and Sandwich Glass Co., 1830-45
Lacy, clear
9¼" D.

Tulip and Acanthus Leaf pattern; eight tulips in base and four in shoulder. Serrated rim.

Robertson and Thornton Antiques
Doylestown, Pa.

32-2 Bowl with Wooden Model
Boston and Sandwich Glass Co., 1850-60
Clear
8" D.

Inverted Heart pattern bowl identical to 17-0. A wooden model was used to create a mold, probably of iron; brass was often used earlier for a mold.

Bennington Museum

32-3 Serving bowl
Pittsburgh area, 1890s
Clear, non-flint
3" H., 8½" D.

Daisy pattern; octagonal paneled bowl with sawtooth rim.

Bennington Museum

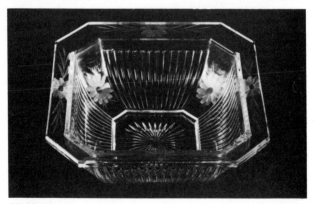

32-4 Bowl
A. H. Helsey & Co., Newark, Ohio, Early 1900s
Crystal
3" H., 8¾" D.

Unidentified ribbed pattern bowl with etched floral decoration; signed Heisey.

Ren's Antiques
Newtown, Pa.

32-5 Cracker Bowl
M'Kee and Brothers, Pittsburgh
1871
Clear
8" D.

Crystal pattern cracker bowl; one of two sizes, 8" and 10", produced for hotel/institutional use by M'Kee. Hexagonal stem and round base. The cover is of tin. As illustrated in the 1871 M'Kee catalogue.

32-6 Footed Bowl
M'Kee and Brothers, Pittsburgh
1871
Clear
8" D.

Crystal pattern serving bowl available in 8" and 10" D. The form and design differs considerably from that seen in 32-5, with a scalloped rim and a prism pattern appearing on the underside of the bowl. Clear only. This pattern has no match among the Eastern glassmakers of the period. As illustrated in the 1871 M'Kee catalogue.

32-7 Footed Bowl
M'Kee and Brothers, Pittsburgh
1871
Clear, non-flint
8" D.

New Pressed Leaf pattern, unique to M'Kee and first introduced in 1868. Two different sizes were produced—8" and 7"—and two forms —low footed and high footed (as illustrated here) were available. The bowls were also offered with covers with acorn finials. Clear only. From the 1871 M'Kee catalogue.

32-8 Footed Bowl
M'Kee and Brothers, Pittsburgh
1871
Clear
8" D.

Rustic pattern low-footed bowl, available with or without cover, as high-foot or low-foot. The low-foot standard base repeats the design of the bowl itself; the high-foot stem is octagonal and formed in a different manner (see 32-7). As illustrated in the 1871 M'Kee catalogue.

33 | Berry Dishes

Bowls used for serving berries are a mid- to late-19th-century form. They differ little from other large bowls of the period, although many of this special type have scalloped or jagged rims. Smaller dishes, in the same pattern as the bowl, were often made available for individual servings. Nappies could be used for berries or other desserts, and are sometimes handled, unlike the bowls. The term "nappy," however, was used somewhat indiscriminately. The examples illustrated in the King, Son & Co. catalogue (33-4) would be recognized simply as bowls by almost any collector.

The mounted berry bowl (33-0) is typical of those offered by silver-plate companies in the 1880s and '90s. Pickle jars and various types of casters were often supplied with plated carriers. These impressive fixtures were not very expensive and made handling at the table much easier.

33-O Berry Bowl and Silver-Plated Basket and Spoon (color plate)
Maker unknown, 1880s
Blue, non-flint
8½" W.

Sequoia pattern, boat-shaped bowl with clear panels. Silver-plate maker is Middletown (Conn.) Silver Plate Co.

Ren's Antiques
Newtown, Pa.

33-1 Nappy
Maker unknown, 1880s-90s
Clear, non-flint
2¼" H., 6" W. with handle

Unidentified rosette and fan pattern; starburst on base. Scalloped rim.

Ren's Antiques
Newtown, Pa.

33-2 Berry Bowl
Maker unknown, 1880s
Blue, non-flint
8½" D.

Raindrop pattern bowl with scalloped rim and round hollow base. Also available in amber, yellow, clear, and apple green.

Robertson and Thornton Antiques
Doylestown, Pa.

33-3 Berry Bowl
Maker unknown, 1880s-90s
Clear, non-flint
5" D.

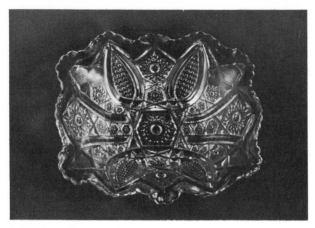

Paneled bowl in unidentified pattern. Imitative of cut glass.

Ren's Antiques
Newtown, Pa.

33-4 Nappies
King, Son & Co., Pittsburgh, Pa., 1870s
Clear, non-flint
Diameters: 3½", 4", 5", 7", and 8"

Bleeding Heart or Floral Ware pattern, Old Set; King also offered a New Set, little different from the Old, in the early 1870s. A nappy or bowl could be used in many different ways, and this design was also offered in a six-inch form with cover. It is thought that Sandwich also produced a similar pattern. As illustrated in a King, Son & Co. (Cascade Glass Works) catalogue from the early 1870s.

34 | Cups and Mugs

Cups for drinking made during the flint-glass period are extremely difficult to find, yet we know that they once existed. The most common form seen today are the miniature lacy cup-and-saucer sets, and presumably, larger versions of these, as well as early patterned pieces, were made before the Civil War. Neither cups nor mugs, however, are listed with any regularity in the lists of flint patterns. Only a Horn of Plenty pattern piece, 34-1, is shown here.

All of the other examples illustrated are post-1860s products made according to some non-flint formula. Many pieces were probably not used for drinking, but as dessert cups for sherbet or custard. The terms cup and mug are used almost interchangeably; a mug is always handled, and a cup, including that used for dessert, usually has one handle, if not two.

34-O Mug (color plate, left to right)
Pittsburgh area, 1870s
Sapphire blue, non-flint
3¼" H.

Grape and Shield pattern mug, possibly made by Doyle & Co., Pittsburgh.

Cup
Maker unknown, 1870s-80s
Clear, non-flint
3¾" H.

Ashburton pattern cup in one of the so-called Colonial designs used throughout the 19th century.

Cup
Attributed to Bryce Brothers, Pittsburgh, 1870s
Clear, non-flint
3⅜" H.

Unidentified bird and tree design cup with rope handle.

Mug
Pittsburgh area, 1880s
Clear, non-flint
3⅜" H.

Roman Rosette (late) pattern mug with applied handle. This design was first produced by Bryce, McKee & Co. (c. 1875) and reissued by U. S. Glass Co. in 1892 and 1898.

Mug
Pittsburgh area, 1870s-80s
Amber, non-flint
3" H.

Hobnail pattern mug of the sort made by many Pittsburgh-area firms; incorporates a rope handle.

Bennington Museum

34-1 Mug
Boston and Sandwich Glass Co.
1850s
Clear
3" H.

Horn of Plenty pattern cup with applied handle; same size as whiskey tumbler in this pattern.

Bennington Museum

34-2 Mug
Northwood Glass Co., Indiana, Pa., 1880s
Opaque custard glass, non-flint
3" H.

Unidentified pattern mug in opaque yellow or custard glass with eight panels, four with bird designs and four with flowers.

Bennington Museum

34-3 Handled Cups
Pittsburgh area, 1890s
Clear with ruby stain, non-flint
Left, 3⅜" H., right, 3" H.

On left, unidentified grapevine design with beaded band. Right, Barreled Block pattern with inscription "To J. McCormack, Clothier, 1894."

The pattern is also known as Red Black. It was made by Gem Model Flint Glass Co., Findlay, Ohio (1890-97), Doyle & Co., Pittsburgh (c. 1885), Fostoria Glass Co., Moundsville, Ohio (c. 1890), and reissued by U. S. Glass Co., Pittsburgh, in 1892 and 1898.

Bennington Museum

35 | Egg Cups

Egg cups, termed holders by almost every manufacturer except M'Kee and Brothers, are among the most attractive and collectible of pressed glass objects. They were some of the earliest items to be pressed and therefore come in a great variety of designs and finishes. By the end of the century use of egg cups had declined greatly, and the practice has only revived slightly since that time. Those used to-day are usually ceramic.

An egg cup with its original cover is a great prize; many holders, however, may never have been supplied with a top for keeping an opened egg warm. Rarely was a cup provided with a handle, as in 35-2. The most colorful examples are from the 1840s and '50s, and feature such shades as opaque blue, opaque apple green, grease blue, electric blue, and opalescent. As with other pressed glass forms, pieces were often made for special customers, and so marked for resale by them. The egg cup (35-3) with the embossed name "Phalon and Son," a New York firm, is one such example.

35-O Egg Cups (color plate, left to right)
Boston and Sandwich Glass Co., 1850s
Opaque blue, opaque apple green, grease blue, and electric blue
All approx. 3⅝" H. if without cover; 5⅜" H. if with cover

Far left and second from left, Bull's-Eye and Bar pattern; remaining cups, Bull's-Eye pattern. Both patterns are most commonly found in clear rather than colored glass.

Bennington Museum

35-1 Egg Cup
New England or Pittsburgh area
1840s
Opalescent
3½" H.

Ashburton pattern cup with hexagonal stem and circular foot.

Bennington Museum

35-2 Handled Egg Cup
Boston and Sandwich Glass Co.
c. 1860
Clear
3⅝" H.

Gothic pattern cup in rarely found handled form; hexagonal stem and circular base.

Bennington Museum

35-3 Egg Cup
Maker unknown, 1840s
Opaque lime green
3¼" H.

Unidentified fine-ribbed pattern with embossed name "Phalon and Son" on inside of raised shield design to one side.

Bennington Museum

35-4 Egg Cup
Boston and Sandwich Glass Co.
1850s
Clear
3 ⅞ " H.

Horn of Plenty pattern cup with
hexagonal knobbed stem resting
on circular foot.

Bennington Museum

35-5 Pair of Egg Cups
Boston and Sandwich Glass Co., 1860s
Clear
3" H.

New England Pineapple pattern with hexagonal stems tapering to
round feet.

Nancy Olsson Antiques
Durham, Pa.

35-6 Egg Cup
Attributed to Bryce Bros., Pittsburgh, 1850-70
Opaque white
3½" H.

Bull's-Eye variant or Texas
Bull's-Eye pattern with tapering
hexagonal stem and circular foot.

Bennington Museum

35-7 Egg Cup
Possibly Boston and Sandwich
   Glass Co., 1870s
Clear, non-flint
3½" H.

Grape Bunch pattern with hexagonal stem and round foot.

Ren's Antiques
Newtown, Pa.

36 | Jars

Special pressed glass jars or pots made for holding mustard, pickles,
marmalade, jelly, or other preparations are a product of the late 19th
century. These are fairly large containers and not meant for preserv-
ing purposes; rather, they are decorative objects that could be
displayed at the table with pride. Some of the containers, as with 36-0,
came with a silver-plated carrier or holder.

The marble or slag glass jars made principally by Challinor, Taylor
& Co. are highly collectible. It was once thought that these variegated pieces were only experimental, produced by workmen after
hours with leftover batches of molten liquid. For this reason, the ware
was termed "End of the Day." The truth is that these pieces, at first
blown-molded and then pressed according to a special technique
patented by David Challinor in 1886, were regularly produced in a
wide assortment of forms. The covered dishes with the distinctive swan
finial are among the most handsome. Three different pattern sets
were produced by Challinor: No. 23, Stylized Flower; No. 13, Fluted;

and No. 28, Oval Set. Similar pieces were produced in England at the time; thses can be distinguished from the American by English registry marks.

36-O Mustard Jar (color plate)
Maker unknown, 1880-1900
Blue, non-flint
Jar, 4½" H.; 10" H. to top of holder

Daisy and Button pattern mustard jar or pot with silver-plate hinged top and carrier.

Bennington Museum

36-1 Pickle Jar
Challinor, Taylor & Co., Tarentum, Pa., 1870s-80s
Marble glass, yellow and white
7" H., 4" D.

Covered marble or slag glass jar with swan finial manufactured under the trade name of "Mosaic." Other colors available were purple and white, opaque blue, and blue and white. Purple and white appears to be the most common.

Bennington Museum

36-2 Pickle Jar
King, Son & Co., Pittsburgh
1870s
Clear, non-flint
Size unknown

No. 14 pattern jar with cover; the diamond and fluted pattern is heavily stippled. King illustrated twenty-six pieces of tableware—including footed bowls, oval bowls, nappies, butter dishes, pitchers, a spoon holder, a wine, and a goblet—in a catalogue dating from the early 1870s. The pattern was available frosted and non-frosted.

36-3 Marmalade Jar
Campbell, Jones & Co.
Pittsburgh, 1870s-80s
Crystal
6" H., 3¼" D.

Covered jam or marmalade
jar in Barley pattern.

Bennington Museum

37 | **Shakers**

Shakers were first used for pepper, since salt was served from small
dishes throughout much of the 19th century, and on formal occasions
today may still be made available in dishes or cellars. It is possible
that salt shakers were intended—at least when first offered in the 1860s
and '70s—for use in the kitchen only. Their convenience is obvious,
especially in preparing food. When dining etiquette became more
relaxed in the 1890s, shakers for both salt and pepper were used more
widely. The tops are threaded to accommodate pierced metal
(usually tinned) heads.

According to Lee, among the late pressed patterns in which the col-
lector may be fortunate to find sets of shakers—in addition to the
Shrine (37-1) and Hobnail (37-2) examples shown here—are Pleat and
Panel, Shell and Tassel, Fish Scale, Roman Rosette, Thousand-Eye,
Two-Panel, Wheat and Barley, Inverted Thumbprint, Willow Oak,
Ribbed Opal Glass, Ruby Thumbprint, Red Block, Moon and Star,
Rosette, Peacock Feather, Daisy and Button, Beaded Grape, Fluted
Ribbon, Beaded Dewdrop, Teardrop and Tassel, Jewel with Dewdrop,
Loops with Dewdrop, Flattened Hobnail, English Hobnail, Three-Face,
Frosted Circle, Curtain, Liberty Bell, Wildflower, Paneled Daisy, Maine,
and Double Loop. It was often common to offer both salt shakers and

dishes in a given pattern, a practice that was followed with a number of the aforementioned sets. Shakers, nonetheless, remain rare.

37-O Pair of Shakers (color plate)
Boston and Sandwich Glass Co., c. 1865
Cobalt blue
4½" H.

Paneled pepper shakers, each threaded to receive a pierced tin top.

Robertson and Thornton Antiques
Doylestown, Pa.

37-1 Salt and Pepper
Midwestern, 1880s
Clear, non-flint
3¼" H., 2" D.

Shrine pattern shakers, threaded to receive pierced tin tops. Available in clear only.

Ren's Antiques
Newtown, Pa.

37-2 Salt and Pepper

Maker unknown, 1880s-90s
Clear, non-flint
4" H.

Hobnail pattern shakers with pattern on bases, as well as sides; threaded with pierced tin tops.

Ren's Antiques
Newtown, Pa.

37-3 Salt Shakers
King, Son & Co., Pittsburgh
1870s
Clear, non-flint
Sizes unknown

Left, footed salt duster; right, "All Right" individual salt shaker. King, Son & Co. illustrated these two shaker forms with twenty-six conventional salt containers, master and individual, without tops. From a catalogue dating from the early 1870s.

38 | Toothpick Holders and Match Holders

Toothpick holders and match holders in pressed glass are special items not frequently encountered by the collector. They usually measure approximately two-and-a-half inches high, and almost all of them were made in the late 19th or early 20th century. They are not listed as part of Victorian pattern-glass sets, but were extras that could be picked up for a cheap price. Some of the holders take an unusual form, as does the object illustrated in 38-3. Those clearly made as novelty items—with hats, boots, and slippers serving as the receptacle—are featured in chapter 49. Other holders appear to have been intended for use in various ways—for toothpicks, matches, or other small items. The Daisy and Button pattern (38-0 and 38-2) was probably a familiar one for such objects.

38-0 Toothpick Holder (color plate)
Maker unknown, 1880-1900
Canary, non-flint
2⅜" H., 3" D.

Daisy and Button pattern holder with three lines dividing the half-inch fold-over rim and body.

Ren's Antiques
Newtown, Pa.

38-1 Toothpick Holder
Maker unknown, 1890s
Clear, non-flint
2½" H., 2⅛" D.

Unidentified paneled pattern imitative of cut glass; scalloped rim and round foot.

Ren's Antiques
Newtown, Pa.

38-2 Match Holder
Maker unknown, 1880-1900
Blue, non-flint
2⅝" H., 2" D.

Daisy and Button pattern holder with nickel-plated bands on top and bottom.

Bennington Museum

38-3 Combination Toothpick Holder and Salt and Pepper
Maker unknown, Early 1900s
Clear, non-flint
1⅞" H., 4⅝" W.

Novelty item held together by center glass pin. The receptacles for salt and pepper are on the bottom.

Ren's Antiques
Newtown, Pa.

39 | Spoon Holders

A holder for spoons is a form which derived from the spill holder in the mid-19th century, although the spoon holder is usually taller and has a longer stem than the earlier form. Most often the rim is scalloped or has a sawtooth edge. A large number of spoons were needed at the typical Victorian table and it made sense to make them available in a holder for use with various courses, or with coffee or tea. So essential was the spoon holder that it was one of only four pieces usually included in the first tableware sets, the others being a sugar bowl, a creamer, and butter dish.

Spoon holders can be found in most of the hundreds of pattern-glass designs which were popular after the Civil War. Illustated here are such patterns as the Blackberry or Bradford Blackberry (39-0 and 39-2), Cable and Fan (39-4), Mosaic (39-6), Good Luck or Horseshoe (39-7), and Emerald Green Herringbone (39-8). They range in size from 4¾ to 6 inches high.

Although not generally used since the early 20th century, spoon holders remain a practical item, as well as a decorative one. Because of the great number made, they are highly collectible today.

39-0 Spoon Holder (color plate)
New England, 1860s
Clear
4¾" H.

Blackberry pattern, also known as Bradford Blackberry or Bradford Grape. The stem is unusually short; scalloped rim.

Robertson and Thornton Antiques
Doylestown, Pa.

39-1 Spoon Holder
Boston and Sandwich Glass Co.
1850s
Clear
5" H.

Sandwich Star pattern; hexagonal body and foot. Rarely found in color.

Bennington Museum

39-2 Spoon Holder
New England, 1860s
Clear
4¾" H.

Identical to 39-0.

Nancy Olsson Antiques
Durham, Pa.

39-3 Spoon Holder
Boston and Sandwich Glass Co.
1860s
Clear
6" H.

Cable and Fan pattern spooner;
each of the six panels is topped
with the fan design which forms
the scalloped rim.

Ren's Antiques
Newtown, Pa.

39-4 Spoon Holder
George Duncan & Sons, Pitts-
**   burgh, 1880s**
Clear
6½" H.

Pittsburgh Tree of Life with Hand
pattern, similar to that produced
earlier by the Portland Glass Co.
The hand, unique to the Pittsburgh
version, forms part of the stem.

Bennington Museum

39-5 Spoon Holder
Maker unknown, 1870s-80s
Opalescent, with canary
**   shading**
4¾" H.

Unidentified basket weave pattern. Overlapping grape or maple leaves form the scalloped rim.

Bennington Museum

39-6 Spoon Holder
Challinor, Taylor & Co., Tarentum, Pa., 1870s-80s
Marble glass, yellow and white
5" H.

Marble or slag glass holder sold under the trade name of "Mosaic." Other colors were available (see 36-1).

Bennington Museum

39-7 Spoon Holder
Adams & Co., Pittsburgh, 1880s
Clear, non-flint
4¾" H., 4¼" D.

Good Luck or Horseshoe pattern holder; the spooner, like the goblet, is without a good luck symbol. Clear only.

Bennington Museum

39-8 Spoon Holder
Maker unknown, 1880s-90s
Emerald green, non-flint
4⅞" H.

Emerald Green Herringbone pattern holder with scalloped rim; not to be confused with an earlier Herringbone pattern which was more highly decorated. Also available in clear.

Bennington Museum

40 | Cruets and Bottles

Cruets have long been made of glass, but, like various bottle forms, are usually blown or blown-molded rather than pressed. Cruets are often found in sets, and are equipped with a stopper, frequently of a cut variety rather than pressed. Use of these narrow-necked pitchers continues to this day in restaurants.

Caster bottles are often found in sets and have metal tops of various types—pewter, Britannia ware, and tinned iron. The term caster is also used for the stand containing such bottles, and in the late Victorian period most caster stands were of silver plate. The bottles were used for holding oil, vinegar, prepared mustard, and other condiments at the table. The stand was usually equipped with a handle so it could be passed easily; the holder might revolve in the manner of a lazy Susan to bring the desired item close at hand.

Other types of bottles—decanters and bar bottles in particular—were also pressed or, as in the case of the Horn of Plenty decanter (40-2), made up of pressed and molded parts.

40-O Cruet (color plate)
Pittsburgh area, 1880s-90s
Blue, non-flint
7" H. with stopper, 3" D.

Block and Star pattern cruet; pattern name is also referred to as Valencia Waffle. Also available in canary, clear, and amber.

Bennington Museum

40-1 Caster Bottle
Maker unknown, 1890s
Clear, non-flint
5¼" H. including top

Unidentified pattern; top is of pewter.

Ren's Antiques
Newtown, Pa.

40-2 Caster Bottle
Maker unknown, 1890s
Clear, non-flint
7¼" H. including top

From the same caster set as 40-1; pewter top.

Ren's Antiques
Newtown, Pa.

40-3 Decanter
Boston and Sandwich Glass Co., 1860s
Clear
8½" H. without stopper; 11⅜" H. with stopper

Horn of Plenty pattern decanter
with molded top and octagonal
pressed bottom. Diamond Point
pattern stopper is not original. Decanters in this pattern with the original stopper are rarely found.

Bennington Museum

40-4 Cruet
Maker unknown, 1880-1900
Clear, non-flint
6¼" H. including stopper

Unidentified pattern cruet with cut
stopper.

Ren's Antiques
Newtown, Pa.

40-5 Cruet
Maker unknown, 1870-90
Clear, non-flint
6¼" H. including stopper

Inverted Heart pattern cruet with cut stopper.

Ren's Antiques
Newtown, Pa.

40-6 Bar Bottle
Pittsburgh area, 1850s
Clear
11" H. without stopper

Pillar and Bull's-Eye pattern bottle with pewter stopper. Possibly made by Bakewell, Pears & Co. as part of the "Thistle" line of glassware. Lee cites two decanters having been made—the "Thistle Straight Decanter" and the "Thistle Cone Decanter," this object having a cone shape. Clear only.

Nancy Olsson Antiques
Durham, Pa.

41 | Tumblers

Water tumblers are among the easiest items for the collector to concentrate on finding. These "glasses," made at a time when water was not served in 5½-to-6-inch vessels and soft drinks were unknown, vary in size from 3½ to 4½ inches. The footed variety (41-3, 41-6 and 41-7) are naturally the largest. Tumblers were often available in sets, as are water glasses today.

Tumblers are found in the earliest pressed glass patterns such as Horn of Plenty (41-0), New England Pineapple (41-0), Diamond Thumbprint (41-1), Excelsior with Maltese Cross (41-2), Early Moon and Star (41-3), Flute (41-5), and Morning Glory (41-7). Whiskey and other bar tumblers of a smaller size are not included here, but are documented in chapter 46. The Flute pattern was commonly used for these bar wares produced by glass manufacturers everywhere in the East and Middle West from the mid-1800s to today.

The later water tumblers in non-flint glass partake of many more designs and forms than the earlier flint objects. In general, they are also more colorful. Two of the most interesting types are the custard glass products of the Indiana Tumbler and Goblet Co. (41-8) from the first decade of the 1900s, and the ruby-stained tumblers (41-11) produced by such Pittsburgh-area firms as Adams & Co., and the O'Hara Glass Co., from the 1870s on. Many of these later patterns were continued by the United States Glass Co.

41-0 Tumblers (color plate, far left)
Maker unknown, 1880s-90s
Amber, non-flint
3⅝" H.

Inverted Thumbprint pattern body and Daisy and Button pattern base. Also available in yellow, blue, green, and clear.

Tumblers (second from left and second from right)
Boston and Sandwich Glass Co., 1860s
Clear
4" H.

New England Pineapple pattern; from a water set of four tumblers.

Tumblers (third from left and third from right)
Boston and Sandwich Glass Co., 1850s
Clear
3¾" H.

Horn of Plenty pattern; from a water set of four tumblers. According to Lee, reproductions in amber have been made.

Tumbler (fourth from left)
Pittsburgh area, 1880s-90s
Yellow, non-flint
4⅛" H.

Finecut and Panel pattern. Made by several Pittsburgh firms and reissued by U. S. Glass after the 1890s merger. Also available in amber, blue, and clear.

Tumbler (fifth from left)
Pittsburgh area, 1880s-90s
Blue, non-flint
3¾" H.

Honeycomb and Rib pattern in a light color popular in the late 19th century.

Tumbler (far right)
Hartley and Co., Tarentum, Pa., 1880s
Amber, non-flint
3⅝" H.

Three-Panel pattern; also available in canary, blue, and clear.

Bennington Museum

41-1 Tumbler
Boston and Sandwich Glass Co.
1840s-50s
Clear
3¾" H.

Diamond Thumbprint pattern; band of oval impressions at top.

Nancy Olsson Antiques
Durham, Pa.

41-2 Tumblers
Attributed to M'Kee Bros., Pittsburgh, 1850s
Clear
3" H.

Set of four tumblers in the Excelsior with Maltese Cross pattern. The cross is found within each of the diamonds.

Robertson and Thornton Antiques
Doylestown, Pa.

41-3 Footed Tumbler
Boston and Sandwich Glass Co.
1850s
Clear
4¼" H.

Early Moon and Star pattern;
round foot. Not to be confused
with later (1880s) Moon and Star
design in non-flint glass.

Nancy Olsson Antiques
Durham, Pa.

41-4 Footed Tumbler
Bakewell, Pears and Co., Pitts-
burgh, 1850s
Amethyst
4" H.

Flute pattern with eight gently ar-
ching flutes or panels; set on octagonal foot.

Bennington Museum

41-5 Tumblers

New England area, 1850s-60s
Left, cobalt blue; right, light amethyst
Left, 3⅜" H.; right, 3¼" H.

Both objects are in the Flute pattern. The tumbler on the left is hexagonal; the tumbler on the right is octagonal. The flutes or panels are very gently arched.

Bennington Museum

41-6 Footed Tumbler
Pittsburgh area, 1850s-60s
Cobalt blue
4⅞" H.

Unidentified paneled and framed oval and crescent pattern; gradually tapering hexagonal stem and foot.

Nancy Olsson Antiques
Durham, Pa.

41-7 Footed Tumbler
Boston and Sandwich Glass Co.
1860s
Clear
4¾" H.

Morning Glory pattern tumbler; circular foot and stem.

Bennington Museum

41-8 Tumbler
Indiana Tumbler and Goblet Co.,
Greentown, Ind., Early 1900s
Shades of brown

4" H.

Marble or slag glass in Cactus pattern.

Bennington Museum

41-9 Tumbler
Boston and Sandwich
  Glass Co., 1880s
Clear, non-flint
3¾" H.

Chrysanthemum Leaf pattern, one of the last to have been made before the closing of the Sandwich plant in 1888.

Bennington Museum

41-10 Tumblers
Pittsburgh area, 1880s
Cranberry, non-flint
3⅝" H.

Inverted Thumbprint pattern, sometimes referred to as Coin Dot. The shade of red was one of the most popular colors near the end of the century.

Nancy Olsson Antiques
Durham, Pa.

41-11 Tumbler
Pittsburgh area, 1893
Clear and ruby stained, non-flint
3 ⅞ " H.

York Herringbone pattern tumbler;
inscribed "World's Fair/1893".

Bennington Museum

42 | Goblets

A careful study of pressed glass goblets can reveal more about the extent of 19th-century pattern ware production than can the examination of any other form. The goblet was executed in almost every possible design. For this reason, such authorities as Alice Hulett Metz and Dr. S. T. Millard have depended on examples of these objects to illustrate the particulars of pressed glass production. The collector, however, should be aware that a particular goblet design may not be representative of that found on other forms in the same pattern category. In addition, goblets are among the most widely reproduced items in the 20th century, and is often very difficult to detect a fake from among the over one thousand legitimate patterns, particularly those in a non-flint glass.

A number of the items illustrated in this chapter are to be found in maufacturers' catalogues or come with impeccable credentials. Notable among these are the Vernon Honeycomb pattern goblet shown with a wooden model used for making the Sandwich mold (42-4), and an Oval and Fine Pleat pattern goblet and wooden model (42-10). The latter pattern was probably one of the last produced by Sandwich in the 1880s.

The goblets illustrated here vary in size from 5¼ to 6¼ inches, a range which seems to be representative of the form in general. Flint glass goblets of the pre-Civil War period tend to be slightly larger than those of the lime-glass era. Color appears to be more common in the later period.

Included in this category is one handled goblet (42-1) produced by Sandwich. If the reader knows of any other example, please contact this writer or the Bennington Museum immediately. The piece appears to be unique.

42-O Goblet (color plate)
Midwestern area, 1870s-80s
Clear, non-flint
5¼" H.

Blackberry pattern goblet with plain stem tapering to a round foot.

Robertson and Thornton Antiques
Doylestown, Pa.

42-1 Handled Goblet
Boston and Sandwich Glass Co.
1840s-50s
Clear
6¼" H.

Flat Diamond and Panel goblet;
"Forget Me Not" is engraved in
one panel. Considered to be a
presentation piece, and may be
a unique example. Pattern also
available in opaque colors.

Bennington Museum

42-2 Goblet
Bakewell, Pears and Co.,
**   Pittsburgh, 1840s-50s**
Clear
6¼" H.

Giant Prism and Thumbprint pattern; flaring goblet with knob stem
tapering to a plain round foot.

Nancy Olsson Antiques
Durham, Pa.

42-3 Goblet
Attributed to Boston and Sand-
     wich Glass Co., c. 1850
Clear
5¾" H.

Flaring Grooved Bigler pattern or
a variation known as Worchester.
The top is exceptionally flared; the
stem is double knobbed.

Ren's Antiques
Newtown, Pa.

42-4 Goblet with Wooden Model
Boston and Sandwich Glass Co., 1850s
Clear
6¼" H.

Vernon Honeycomb pattern goblet with model used in making mold;
the pattern has also been known as Cincinnati. Sandwich also produced another honeycomb design called New York; in this, the

distinctive pattern covered only the lower half of the goblet.

Bennington Museum

42-5 Goblet
Boston and Sandwich Glass Co.
1860s
Clear
6¼" H.

Horn of Plenty pattern goblet with
knobbed and flaring stem ending
in a plain round foot.

Bennington Museum

Stedman Goblet.   R. L. Goblet.   Mirror Goblet.

42-6 Goblet (left)
M'Kee Brothers, Pittsburgh, 1864
Clear
Size unknown

Stedman pattern as illustrated in the 1864 M'Kee catalogue. A similar
pattern, Blaze, was produced by the New England Glass Co. in the late
1860s. Stedman, however, is heavier flint glass and rougher in design
execution; the base of the Stedman goblet is rayed, whereas the base
or foot of the New England type is not.

42-7 Goblet (center)
M'Kee Brothers, Pittsburgh, 1864
Clear
Size unknown

Ribbed Leaf or Bellflower pattern goblet as illustrated in the 1864 M'Kee catalogue. Sandwich referred to its almost identical pattern as Bellflower, and that name is preferred regardless of maker.

42-8 Goblet (right)
M'Kee Brothers, Pittsburgh, 1868
Clear
Size unknown

Mirror pattern goblet illustrated in the 1868 M'Kee catalogue. This is a perfectly round thumbprint design.

42-9 Goblet
Maker unknown, 1870s
Clear
5⅞" H.

Sunburst pattern goblet with tapering hexagonal stem and plain round foot. Also available, but rare, in amber and blue.

Ren's Antiques
Newtown, Pa.

42-10 Goblet with Wooden Model
Boston and Sandwich Glass Co., c. 1880
Clear, non-flint
5¾" H.

Oval and Fine Pleat pattern goblet with model used for producing mold. Octagonal stem and round foot.

Bennington Museum

42-11 Goblet
Maker unknown, 1880s-90s
Clear, non-flint
5¼" H.

Prism and Daisy Bar pattern goblet with octagonal stem and round foot.

Ren's Antiques
Newtown, Pa.

42-12 Goblets
Pittsburgh area, 1880s
Clear, non-flint
6" H.

Leaf and Dart pattern goblets with hexagonal stems and round bases. Possibly produced by Richards and Hartley, Tarentum, Pa., who called the pattern "Pride."

Frenchtown House of Antiques
Frenchtown, N.J.

42-13 Goblet
Midwestern, or Pittsburgh area
1870s-80s
Clear, non-flint
5¼" H.

Deer and Pine Tree pattern; also available in yellow, apple green, and amber. Among the most popular of late pressed glass patterns.

Bennington Museum

42-14 Goblet
Maker unknown, 1880s-90s
Clear, non-flint
5½" H.

Unidentified curved bars pattern
with panels; knobbed stem and
scalloped foot.

Bennington Museum

43 | Champagnes and Clarets

A champagne glass is slightly smaller than a goblet and a bit larger
than a wine or a cordial. The average size would appear to be approximately five inches high. It is difficult, however, to set any hard
and fast rule regarding this somewhat variable form. The distinction
between a wine, a champagne, and a goblet during the 1840-70
period of flint-glass manufacture seems to have been only one of
height; the basic form of the bowl remained the same. The champagne glass does not appear on the lists of most pattern-glass sets of
the last quarter of the century. When it does, it more closely resembles
the flaring shape familiar to us today.

The term "claret" is one that gradually disappeared during the
century as popular taste for this dry red wine, usually a Bordeaux,
declined. In the 1840s and '50s a claret was slightly smaller than a
champagne, but larger than a wine. Its bowl form is identical to that of
a champagne, wine, or goblet.

43-O Champagne Glasses (color plate, far left, second from left, far
    right, and second from right)
Maker unknown, 1880s-90s

Periwinkle blue
5" H.

Four glasses in the very popular Diamond Quilted pattern produced by Eastern, Pittsburgh area, and Midwestern glass factories. Also available in yellow, pale amethyst, deep amethyst, apple green, pale amber, dark amber, and clear. Widely reproduced.

Champagne Glasses (third and fifth from left)
Boston and Sandwich Glass Co., 1860s
Clear
5¼" H.

Horn of Plenty champagne glasses, part of a set of four.

Claret Glass (fourth from left)
Boston and Sandwich Glass Co., 1860s
Clear
4⅞" H.

Horn of Plenty claret glass; flaring top and knob stem.

Bennington Museum

43-1 Champagne Glass
M'Kee Brothers, Pittsburgh, 1864
Clear
Size unknown

New York Honeycomb pattern, referred to by M'Kee simply as the New York pattern. In contrast to the Vernon Honeycomb (see 42-4) produced by Sandwich, the pattern only extends halfway up the goblet. As illustrated in the 1864 M'Kee catalogue.

43-2 Champagne Glass
M'Kee Brothers, Pittsburgh, 1860s
Clear
Size unknown

Sprig or Ribbed Palm pattern champagne glass, the first pattern to be patented by M'Kee in 1863. As illustrated in the 1869 M'Kee catalogue. Clear only.

44 | Wines

Wine glasses were made in small and large sizes with variations occurring in the stem and bowl from the 1840s through the end of the century. The smaller wines, sometimes also termed cordials, vary from 2½ inches to approximately 3½ inches; the larger wines range from 3½ to nearly 5 inches.

Most wine glasses are footed, but tumbler-form wines from late in the 1800s do exist (see 44-7). These may have been meant for tasting or for liqueurs.

Wine glasses are found in almost all the known flint patterns and are included in some non-flint patterned sets. The less frequent appearance of the form through the decades would seem to parallel the declining popularity of wine and the gradual adoption of beer as the standard alcoholic beverage in the American home.

44-O Wine Glasses (color plate)
Maker unknown, 1880s-90s
Periwinkle blue, non-flint
4½" H.

Diamond Quilted pattern wines a half inch smaller in size than those illustrated in 43-0. Other colors available: pale amethyst, dark amethyst, apple green, pale amber, dark amber, and clear.

Bennington Museum

44-1 Cordial
Boston and Sandwich Glass Co.
1850s-60s
Clear
4⅜" H.

Horn of Plenty pattern cordial or liqueur glass; knob and octagonal stem tapering to round foot.

Bennington Museum

44-2 Wine Glass
Maker unknown, 1890s
Clear, non-flint
4" H.

Late Thumbprint pattern wine in barrel shape; tapering octagonal stem.

Ren's Antiques
Newtown, Pa.

44-3 Wine Glass
Boston and Sandwich Glass Co.
1850s-60s
Clear
4⅞" H.

Horn of Plenty pattern wine glasses; identical to 44-2 except in size.

Bennington Museum

44-4 Wine Glass
New England area, 1850s-60s
Clear
4¾" H.

Lee pattern wine glass, a name honoring the pressed glass expert. (See also 29-9)

Ren's Antiques
Newtown, Pa.

44-5 Wine Glass
Bryce, McKee & Co.
  Pittsburgh, Pa., 1880s
Blue, non-flint
4½" H.

Cathedral or Orion pattern wine glass first produced by Bryce, McKee and reissued in 1898 by U. S. Glass. Note unusual banding on stem. Also available in crystal or clear, amber, canary, and amethyst.

Bennington Museum

44-6 Wine Glass
Midwestern area, 1870s-80s
Amber, non-flint
3⅝" H.

Spirea Band pattern wine glass
with knob stem. Also available in
yellow, blue, and apple green.

Bennington Museum

44-7 Cordial or Small Wine Glass
Pittsburgh area, 1902
Ruby stain and clear, non-flint
2⅜" H.

Ruby flash or stain glass in tumbler
form; marked "1902."

Ren's Antiques
Newtown, Pa.

45 | Ale Glasses and Mugs

The growing preference for beer as a daily beverage during the 19th
century created a new market for special glasses and mugs. A signifi-
cant percentage of America's new immigrant population came from
German-speaking areas of Europe where beer or ale was a staple of
the diet. German ale-glass forms (as illustrated in 45-5) were added to

those of the English tradition. Many pressed glass manufacturers probably produced more items for the bar and hotel market than for home use during the last four decades of the 19th century. The King, Son and Co. catalogue from the 1870s, for example, illustrates twenty-seven different ale glasses and twenty-one beer mugs; some of the mugs were engraved with such mottos as "Gut Heil" and "Gesundheit".

Traditional pressed ale glasses of the Anglo-American variety were produced in flint by Eastern and Midwestern factories fairly early in the century. These were available in a limited number of patterns such as Thumbprint or Argus (45-1), Bigler (45-2), and Brooklyn or Giant Prism and Thumbprint (45-3). Most ale glasses are very simple in design and were not offered as part of the patterned sets which became popular in the 1860s and '70s. The Flute pattern was used for the majority of pieces, as it was for bar ware in general.

Commemorative and political designs began to appear on mugs in the 1880s. Whether these items were used for beer drinking or not is unknown; the choice may have depended on the voter. The highly decorative mugs were probably used as much for display as for drinking.

45-O Mug (color plate, left to right)
Maker unknown , 1896
Frosted glass
3½" H.

Frosted portrait mug of the 1896 Democratic candidate for president. The inscription reads "The Peoples Money/Wm. J. Bryan". Although not designated a beer mug, which was ordinarily a larger object, its use for this purpose was likely; victory, however, was not to be celebrated by Bryan and his followers.

Ale Glass
Maker unknown, 1850s-60s
Clear
8⅝" H.

New York Honeycomb pattern known to have been produced in both the Pittsburgh and New York areas. In this pattern the motif appears only in the lower half of the article. This object has also been identified as a celery, a description which cannot be disproved, but it seems more likely that the use is as indicated here.

Mug
Maker unknown, 1896
Frosted glass
3½" H.

Frosted portrait mug of the 1896 Republican candidate for president. The inscription reads, "Protection and Prosperity/Maj. Wm. McKinley".

Bennington Museum

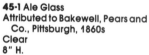

45-1 Ale Glass
Attributed to Bakewell, Pears and
Co., Pittsburgh, 1860s
Clear
8" H.

Thumbprint or Argus pattern ale glass; the design is made up of horizontal ovals, distinguishing it from either round or vertical oval prints. Bakewell, Pears offered the pattern under the Argus name.

Nancy Olsson Antiques
Durham, Pa.

45-2 Ale Glass
Pittsburgh area, 1850s
Clear
6¼" H.

Bigler pattern ale glass with ribbing between panels. This may have been produced by M'Kee and Brothers. Hexagonal in form with round foot.

Nancy Olsson Antiques
Durham, Pa.

45-3 Ale Glass
Possibly Bakewell, Pears and Co.,
   Pittsburgh, 1850s-60s
Clear
6¾" H.

Brooklyn or Giant Prism and
Thumbprint pattern ale glass;
Brooklyn was the trade name
under which the ware was sold.

Nancy Olsson Antiques
Durham, Pa.

45-4 Ale Glass (left)
M'Kee and Brothers, Pittsburgh, 1860s
Clear
Size unknown

Excelsior pattern ale glass, known to have been made as early as
1859. As illustrated in the 1864 M'Kee catalogue.

45-5 Footed Schoppen Ale Glass (right) **and English Ale Glass** (center)
King, Son and Co., Pittsburgh, 1870s
Clear
Sizes unknown

These were standard forms produced by King and other Pittsburgh-
area glass companies following the Civil War. As illustrated in the 1870
King catalogue.

46 | Whiskey Tasters, Flips, and Tumblers

If beer was America's favorite low-alcohol beverage in the post-Civil War period, whiskey was the country's hard liquor equivalent in popularity. The strongly fermented drink was well established during the colonial period, but became even more popular on the Western frontier. Tasters, flips, and tumblers were essential vessels for its enjoyment.

The taster, the smallest of the three forms, is usually not found to be more than two inches high. Those illustrated in color (46-0) are all one-and-three-quarter inches. The flip, often more commonly used for a hot drink than for whiskey, is only slightly larger than a taster. The standard tumbler measures from two to three inches. Those that are footed, as 46-1, are somewhat larger.

Almost all whiskey glasses are fluted, simple pieces of bar ware. The patterned pieces such as 46-1 in the Framed Ovals design or the Horn of Plenty design, 46-3, are among the exceptions. Because so many pieces were produced in the 19th century, however, it is not as difficult as it would seem to find decorative whiskey tumblers of various sizes. The beautifully colored tasters made by the early flint manufacturers are especially prized and these tiny objects can bring very large prices today.

46-0 Whiskey Tasters (color plate)
Boston and Sandwich Glass Co., 1840s
Emerald, lacy, opalescent, clear, amethyst, olive, canary, blue, blue green, light amethyst
Each 1¾" H.

Each in the same unidentified stippled pattern. According to Lee, these are found in "any of the many shades of color used at Sandwich."

Bennington Museum

46-1 Footed Whiskey
Boston and Sandwich Glass Co., or New England area, 1840s
Clear, with gilt trim
4" H.

Framed Ovals pattern in hexagonal form; one of the earliest flint glass patterns.

Nancy Olsson Antiques
Durham, Pa.

46-2 Whiskey
Boston and Sandwich Glass Co.
1850s-60s
Cobalt blue
2¼" H.

Flute pattern in octagonal form; other whiskey or bar tumblers were also produced in six- and nine-flute forms by Sandwich, as well as by almost all glass manufacturers.

Nancy Olsson Antiques
Durham, Pa.

46-3 Whiskey Tumbler
Boston and Sandwich Glass Co.
1850s
Clear
3" H.

Horn of Plenty pattern whiskey; typical in size and form to those available in pattern sets from the mid-century on.

Bennington Museum

46-4 Whiskey Tumbler
M'Kee and Brothers, Pittsburgh
1860s
Clear
Size unknown

Bigler pattern in half-pint size. As illustrated in the 1868 M'Kee catalogue.

47 | Boudoir Accessories

Nearly every collector of pressed glass would like to be able to find an example of an early Sandwich cologne bottle, especially one with its original stopper. Produced during the 1840s, '50s, and '60s, these heavy flint-glass bottles are almost always hexagonal in form and come in a wide variety of colors—canary, emerald green, opaque white, opaque blue—as well as clear. The designs, as Ruth Webb Lee has explained in a chapter on perfume bottles and jars in **Sandwich Glass**, are often the same as those used for lamps, bowls, spill holders, and salts. The Star and Punty pattern (47-0) object is typical of this variety.

Just as rare are the cologne bottles produced by other factories, including the New England Glass Co., Sandwich's rival in so many fields. The deep amethyst octagonal example, 47-0, is extremely handsome. It does not appear that the Midwestern factories produced much fancy ware in the pressed manner, although such firms as Bakewell, Pears & Co. were involved in the manufacture of perfumers' and druggists' ware, probably of a blown-molded variety.

Other pressed items for the vanity or dressing table made during the late 19th century are similarly difficult to find. Most of them were blown-molded or cut.

47-O Cologne Bottle (color plate, left)
Boston and Sandwich Glass Co., 1840-45
Canary
4⅝" H.; 6" H. with stopper

Star and Punty pattern; hexagonal, solid stopper. Also available in green, opaque white, opaque blue, and clear.

Cologne bottle (right)
New England Glass Co., Cambridge, Mass., 1860s
Deep amethyst
3¾" H.; 5¹/₁₆" H. with stopper

Unidentified octagonal paneled oval pattern gradually tapering to a scalloped base; hollow hexagonal stopper. Illustrated in the New England Glass Co. catalogue for 1869.

Bennington Museum

47-1 Cologne Bottle
Boston and Sandwich Glass Co.,
1860s
Canary
4½" H.

Unidentified raised and paneled oval pattern, each oval crossed by five horizontal bars; hexagonal form. Stopper missing.

Bennington Museum

47-2 Scent Bottles
Maker unknown, 1880s-90s
Crystal
Left, 4¾" H.; right, 4¼" H.

Paneled scent bottles in fluted form; cut stoppers.

Ren's Antiques
Newtown, Pa.

47-3 Covered Jar
Maker unknown, 1880s-90s
Ruby stained, non-flint
3¾" H., 4" D.

Floral and leaf design covered jar in gilt; base is solidly stained, while cover is predominantly clear.

Bennington Museum

48 | Pomade Jars

Pomade or ointment jars in the Bear or Little Cavalier form are exclusively a product of Sandwich and are very difficult to find today. They are a special type produced in opaque and opalescent colors in the late 1840s and '50s, and as Ruth Webb Lee suggests, were probably inspired by English or European prototypes in pottery.

Two different Bear designs have been discovered by the experts, one featuring a muzzled creature and the other a chained one. The former is represented in 48-0, far left, and the latter in 48-0, second from left. The sizes appear to range from 3¾ inches to 4½ inches high. The tops (heads) are, of course, removable. Many of the examples found today are in rather poor condition, the heads having been chipped or worn.

The Little Cavalier is found in two sizes, that illustrated (48-0, second from right) being the smaller at 3¼ inches. The origin of this design is unknown, but as with the Bear, it probably originated in Europe.

More conventionally shaped pomade or ointment jars were produced by many companies, although the other examples shown here are all attributed to Sandwich. Only the Basket Weave pattern object, 48-2, would appear to be a unique product of that company.

48-O Pomade Jars (color plate, left to right)
Boston and Sandwich Glass Co., c. 1850
Opalescent
2½" H. with cover, 3¾" H.

Bear pomade jar with head, the smallest of four sizes produced by Sandwich in which the animal is muzzled instead of chained.

Pomade Jar
Boston and Sandwich Glass Co., c. 1850
Opaque blue
3¹⁵⁄₁₆" H.; 5⅝" H. with cover

Bear pomade jar with head, crossed paws, and chains; the larger of two sizes produced by Sandwich in which the animal is chained. Object is marked "X BAZIN, PHILADA", and was probably custom made for this outlet.

Pomade Jar
Boston and Sandwich Glass Co., 1850s
Opaque blue
3¼" H.

Little Cavalier jar, small size. Most of these very rare jars are found in opaque white or blue.

Bennington Museum

48-1 Pomade Jar
Boston and Sandwich Glass Co., 1830-35
Clear
3" H.

Simple octagonal pomade or ointment jar with cover; exceptionally fine flint glass in paneled oval design.

Bennington Museum

48-2 Covered Pomade Jar
Boston and Sandwich Glass Co.
1850s
Opaque lime or apple green
2" H.; 3¹⁵/₁₆" H. with cover

Basket Weave pattern jar of considerable luminesence; finial cover.

Bennington Museum

48-3 Pomade Jar
Boston and Sandwich Glass Co.
1850s
Opaque blue
4½ H. with cover

Bear pomade jar with head, the next to smaller of four sizes of the unchained creature; with muzzle.

Bennington Museum

48-4 Pomade Jar
Boston and Sandwich Glass Co.
1850s
Opaque black
3¾" H. with cover

Bear pomade jar with head in a
most unusual color; same size as
first jar from left in 48-0. Muzzled
and not chained.

Bennington Museum

48-5 Ointment Jar
Boston and Sandwich Glass Co., 1860s
Fiery opalescent
2½" D.

Nine-sided jar featuring paneled diamond, oval, and plume designs.
Originally supplied with pewter or tin lid.

Robertson and Thornton Antiques
Doylestown, Pa.

49 | **Novelties**

Items made primarily for their decorative or amusement value were extremely popular in the post-Civil War period. While they might serve some useful purpose (as an ash tray, toothpick holder, drinking glass, bouquet holder, inkwell, shaker), they were not intended to take the place of more conventional objects. Novelty pieces often rested on a knicknack or whatnot shelf rather than on the dining room or bedside table.

The variety of objects is truly astounding. Ruth Webb Lee illustrates over one hundred varieties of pressed slippers, boots, shoes, and roller skates in her definitive **Victorian Glass**. Some, like the high button shoe (49-0, far right), are highly detailed creations; others, such as the clear slipper with gold bow (49-0, second from right) are slight, off-hand whimsies. The Pittsburgh area seems to have been the center of production, although manufacturing also took place in the East.

49-O Toothpick Holder (color plate, left to right)
Probably Pittsburgh area, 1870s-80s
Blue, non-flint
2⅝" H.

Boot-form toothpick holder with star design impressed on bottom of heel.

Bouquet Holder
Pittsburgh area, 1880s-90s
Pink, non-flint
6" H.

Daisy and Button design holder consisting of a hand holding a cornucopia.

Inkwell
Maker unknown, 1870s-80s
Amber, non-flint
2⅞" H.; 3" D. of stand

Plain boot-form container with cover; resting on stand. Cane design appears on cover. Another variety cited by Lee is found in blue and has a cover with a six-pointed ornament.

Slipper
Maker unknown, late 1800s
Crystal
5" L.

Clear slipper with applied, painted gold bow; the use of the object is unknown.

Bouquet Holder
Attributed to Pittsburgh area, 1890s
Purple, non-flint
5¼" H.

High button shoe in the Cane pattern; scrolled base. Base is lettered on one side, "PAT. APPLIED FOR", and on the other, "BOUQUET HOLDER".

Bennington Museum

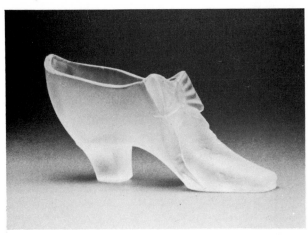

49-1 Slipper
Maker unknown, late 1800s
Frosted, non-flint
4½" L.

Similar to slipper illustrated in 49-0, but cut higher.

Bennington Museum

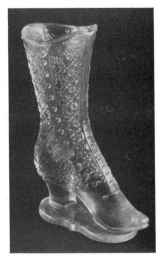

49-2 Bouquet Holder
Attributed to Pittsburgh area
1890s
Electric blue, non-flint
5½" H.

Identical to example illustrated in 49-0, but in a different color.

Bennington Museum

49-3 Roller Skate
United States Glass Co., Pittsburgh, 1890s
Yellow, non-flint
3¾" L.

Slipper/roller skate in the Daisy and Button pattern. Lee mentions that other manufacturers may have produced similar models.

Bennington Museum

49-4 Toothpick Holder
Maker unknown, Late 1800s
Amber
2⅜" H.

Fan-top holder in Daisy and Button pattern. Also produced in a smaller size for use as a salt. Found also in cobalt blue, canary, clear, and light blue.

Bennington Museum

---

50 | Miniatures

Miniature or toy objects were produced throughout the 19th century in both flint and non-flint glass. Almost any one of these pieces, regardless of age, is highly collectible today. They are often charming, sometimes colorful, finely executed scaled-down versions of real-life objects. They were intended to be used as doll house furnishings or simply to be treasured as tiny trinkets.

The most appealing and valuable of the miniatures are the lacy objects from Sandwich and the clear candlestick and the iron from M'Kee and Brothers, illustrated in color (50-0). It is possible that both companies produced clear and lacy miniatures; the attributions are based on evidence from sales catalogues and fragments found in the field. So-called toy sets were also produced by other firms. Related to these pieces are the A.B.C. plates in six-inch diameter and 1.2.3. plates in a four-inch diameter. Miniatures were considered not only amusing objects, but effective pedagogical tools.

50-O Doll Dishes and Other Miniature Objects (color plate, from bowl, top center)
Boston and Sandwich Glass Co., and Pittsburgh area, 1830s-60s
Size of electric blue pitcher, 2¼" H.

Canary bowl, Sandwich

Lacy cup and saucer, Sandwich

Clear spill holder, Sandwich

Opalescent pitcher, Sandwich

Clear candlestick, M'Kee and Brothers, Pittsburgh

Clear iron, M'Kee and Brothers, Pittsburgh

Electric blue pitcher, Sandwich

Canary bowl, Sandwich

(center) Lacy, amethyst tureen and tray, small size, Sandwich

Bennington Museum

50-1 Tureen and Tray
Boston and Sandwich Glass Co., 1830s-40s
Lacy, clear
Tureen, 1⅞" H. with cover; 3" D.

Tray, ⅜"H., 2⅝" D.

Lacy, stippled tureen with fan ornaments on cover and sides; like the tureen illustrated in 50-1, this is the smaller of two kinds produced by Sandwich. The tray has a flower border and a scalloped rim.

Bennington Museum

50-2 Vegetable Dish
Boston and Sandwich Glass Co.
1830s-40s
Lacy, clear
2⅞" L., 2" W.

Lacy, oval vegetable dish with center diamond design; scalloped edge.

Bennington Museum

50-3 Creamer
Midwestern, or Pittsburgh area, 1880s
Clear, non-flint
3" H.

Cut Log pattern, also known as Cat's Eye and Block, and produced by the Greensburg Glass Co. and the Westmoreland Specialty Co.

Bennington Museum

50-4 Punch bowl and Six Handled Cups
Maker unknown, Early 1900s
Clear, non-flint
Punch bowl, 4¼" H., 4⅜" D.; Cups, 1" H., 1½" D.

Tulip and Honeycomb pattern is repeated throughout the set; bowl, base, and cups with applied handles.

Ren's Antiques
Newtown, Pa.

Selected Bibliography

Only those volumes are listed which are currently available from the publisher or can be obtained at most libraries.

Barret, Richard Carter. *Blown and Pressed American Glass.* Manchester, Vt.: Forward's Color Productions, Inc., 1967.

Cooke, Lawrence S., ed. *Lighting in America. From Colonial Rushlights to Victorian Chandeliers.* Antiques Magazine Library. New York: Main Street/Universe Books, 1977.

DiBartolomeo, Robert E., ed. *American Glass From the Pages of Antiques.* Vol. II, Pressed and Cut. Princeton: The Pyne Press, 1974.

Innes, Lowell. *Pittsburgh Glass 1797-1891, A History and Guide for Collectors.* Boston: Houghton Mifflin Co., 1976.

Lee, Ruth Webb. *Early American Pressed Glass.* Revised ed. Wellesley Hills, Mass.: Lee Publications, 1958.

_____. *Sandwich Glass.* Framingham Centre, Mass.: privately published, 1939.

_____. *Victorian Glass.* Wellesley Hills, Mass.: Lee Publications, 1944.

Lee, Ruth Webb, and Rose, James H. *American Glass Cup Plates.* Wellesley Hills, Mass.: Lee Publications, 1948.

McKearin, George S., and McKearin, Helen. *American Glass.* New York: Crown Publishers, 1941.

M'Kee and Brothers. *M'Kee Victorian Glass. Five Complete Glass Catalogs from 1859/60 to 1871.* New York: Dover Publications, Inc. 1981.

Metz, Alice Hulett. *Early American Pattern Glass.* Vol. I. Westfield, N.Y.: The Guide Publishing Co., 1958.

_____. *More Early American Pattern Glass.* Vol II. Chicago: privately published, 1965.

Pennsylvania Glassware, 1870-1904. American Historical Catalog Collection. Princeton: The Pyne Press, 1972.

Revi, Albert Christian. *American Pressed Glass and Figure Bottles.* New York: Thomas Nelson & Sons, 1964.

_____. *Nineteenth-Century Glass.* New York: Thomas Nelson & Sons, 1967.

Wilson, Kenneth M. *New England Glass and Glassmaking.* New York: Crowell, 1972.

Index to Patterns, Designs, and Forms